MARY MATTHEWS FETTERMAN
AND CAPTAIN ALICE J. MATTHEWS, ANC

A STORY OF FAITH AND SERVICE
BEHIND THE FRONT LINE OF WORLD WAR II

ISBN 978-1-66784-223-3 eBook 978-1-66784-224-0

Dedication

I dedicate this book to my Aunt Alice, whose commitment to her military service and to her patients was truly remarkable. This book is also dedicated to the U.S. military medical personnel for their unwavering dedication to the troops they serve, here in the United States and abroad. You are all truly heroes.

PREFACE

This book does not claim to be an account of facts and events, but of the personal experiences of Captain Alice J. Matthews, told in letters written home to family, a memoir written by Alice in 1993 based on those letters, a video interview conducted by Donna Sklar at The Zekelman Holocaust Center, Farmington Hills, Michigan on May 1, 1995, conversations with Alice and family stories remembered about a remarkable woman.

These are Alice's own words, spoken through her letters and her memoir, as this is the most accurate method for you, the reader, to get the true account of her experiences and feelings. This account of Captain Alice J. Matthews follows her from her decision to become a nurse and join the army, to her unwavering service following the U.S. Army, First Division, with the 45th Evacuation Hospital as they entered the European Theater of World War II on Omaha Beach on D-10.

Contents

INTRODUCTION

Alice Jessie Matthews was an ordinary woman who made an extraordinary choice. She, like many women who had become nurses, chose to leave the comfort and normalcy of everyday life. Alice had never traveled more than eight miles from home and she would travel across the Atlantic Ocean to a foreign land, to aid doctors in using their skills to repair the damages of war.

Alice was born in 1918 in Philadelphia, the third child of six, to Scotch/Irish immigrants, Ernest and Matilda Matthews. She grew up in a very close knit, Christian family, full of happiness, love and adventure. Alice's family enjoyed art, writing poetry and horticulture. Ernest and Matilda instilled a strong faith in God and a love of their adopted country in their children.

In 1927, at the age of nine, Alice and her family moved from Philadelphia to a house her father had built on Monument Avenue in Malvern, Pennsylvania, a suburb of Philadelphia. The small town of one square mile was considered then to be 'out in the country'. One could not help but be patriotic growing up on Monument Avenue. The Matthews home was two blocks down from the Paoli Memorials Grounds, the site of The Great Paoli Massacre that happened during the Revolutionary War. Several regiments of the Continental Army, under General Anthony Wayne, were massacred by the British there on September 9, 1777. The battlefield became a preserved memorial park and parade ground with a stone wall enclosed gravesite of 53 American soldiers that lost their lives in that battle. It houses the country's third oldest war monument. The gravesite is flanked by two iron canons that were recovered a century after they were hidden by the British in a Chester County iron forge. The Memorial Grounds were used for training soldiers for the War of 1812, The Mexican War and The Civil War. Every year, since 1868, Malvern has held a Memorial Day parade. It is the oldest, continuously held Memorial

Parade held in America. The Matthews family would sit on their front porch and watch as the parade went by. All the neighbors on Monument Avenue put out their American flags and stood as American veterans from each branch of the military marched by, in formation, carrying their regiment's flag. There were local and state officials, girl and boy scout troops and high school bands that paraded by. Everyone from Malvern and local communities were along the parade route and they would follow the end of the parade up to The Memorial Grounds to listen to the school marching bands that would play The National Anthem, America the Beautiful and John Philip Sousa compilations. Then they would listen to speeches about how great our country was and how much we admired the servicemen and women that selflessly served to ensure our peace, freedoms and our safety. Year after year, the Matthews family followed the parade. How could an immigrant's family not be influenced to yearn to serve their adopted country?

The Matthews family did everything together. The siblings were their own best friends. Alice felt very fortunate and often said she did not realize that all children did not share such memories as part of their childhood. It was a much different time for children growing up then, compared to today. Small things brought such happiness and somehow, even those things were not needed with such an abundance of love and security that Alice's parents provided. The Matthews children were the center of their parents' lives. This is Alice's story.

The Matthews home on Monument Avenue in Malvern, Pennsylvania

The cannons in front of the walled cemetery at the Paoli Memorial Grounds

BECOMING AN ARMY NURSE

After the Matthews family moved from Philadelphia to Malvern, there were many family members who visited often. Alice's favorite visitor was her Aunt Julia. Aunt Julia was a registered nurse at Philadelphia General Hospital, employed as an operating room supervisor.

"She was a wonderful, giving person who was always there for the family through many illnesses – a true Florence Nightingale. We knew if she was there, everything would be alright. She would keep us spellbound with her interesting experiences she had had in her youth and especially her nursing experiences. She was 'just a good person'. Then she introduced us to her friend who had been an Army nurse overseas during World War 1, and a whole new avenue of interest was opened for me. I would not only be a nurse – but an Army nurse!

My sister Julia and I had our first visit to a hospital when our father was in an auto accident. We were permitted to visit our father. The hospital was so big and the smell of disinfectant was so strong! And it was so quiet – everyone seemed to speak in whispers. And, of course, no televisions or radios, and very few visitors. It was as if we were on holy ground! It was quite a shock to see our healthy father lying under a white sheet – his leg in traction and his face all cut with the glass from the windshield. Julia even found glass shards still in his face. But we had seen him and felt somewhat assured that he would be alright in time. And he was – after what seemed like a long time, able to come home with a cast on his leg."

Throughout the 1940's, professional women were few and far between, since the only professional positions that were accepted by mainstream society were typists, secretaries, teachers and nurses. Women were the center of the home, while men were responsible for 'bringing home the bacon'.

"As long as I could remember, I had wanted to become a nurse. No other profession held any appeal for me. There was no question or doubt in my mind that being a nurse would be my first choice."

Alice and her sister Julia entered the three-year nursing program at Chester County Hospital together in 1936. On October 28, 1939, while in their final months of school, their father was brought in as an emergency patient with a cerebral hemorrhage. They both were nurses to him and he passed after just two days there. Upon graduating and becoming Licensed Registered Nurses, Alice became a private duty nurse for almost two years.

"Far away in Europe, there had been increasing rumblings of discord with the rapid rise of a German named Hitler. He was to be the savior of Germany and he had a vast following. Gradually, his army marched into smaller European countries, conquering and cruelly subduing them. Soon, all Europe was being threatened by this Nazi army that seemed invincible. Our allies – Great Britain and France, desperately needed U.S. aid, but The United States tried to remain neutral."

With the coming of war, a vast new spectrum of job opportunities opened, especially in the medical fields. Eager to contribute to the war effort, many young women opted to become military nurses. One of the main obstacles that these women faced on the road to becoming nurses, was informing their parents of their decision to serve. Also, life as a nurse wasn't glamorous and learning to follow strict government orders was a challenge for many women. Life as a nurse, especially in an evacuation hospital, was an entirely new experience for the women who served, and was hard, dangerous work. This was due in part to the technology of the time, blackout periods and the close proximity of the hospital tents to the battles. However, for the women who experienced it, the benefits easily outweighed every minute of hardship.

"Prior to Pearl Harbor, I realized that we would soon have to help our European allies, and I joined the Army Nurse Corps in May, 1941 at the age of 22. I finally had my opportunity to see my dreams become reality. At this time, the U.S. was still a peaceful country and we would not be actively involved in the war for another seven months, when Japan made its attack on Pearl Harbor. Pay as a First Lieutenant started at $50 per month, then was raised to $70, then raised again to $150."

Alice felt the daily fervor of a country on the verge of an all-encompassing war. She felt an excitement and a need to be part of it. All nurses in the military were there on a volunteer basis. Alice was the first from Chester County Hospital to volunteer. It would be a minimum of a two-year commitment. That several classmates, including her sister, Julia, had planned to enter the Army when Alice did, then changed their minds, did not affect her resolve to go ahead with her plans, for she was determined to serve. These same classmates later joined the Navy Nurse Corps.

ORDERS TO REPORT

"When I received my official orders from Army Headquarters to report to New Orleans, Louisiana, I could not accept that, for I had requested either of two posts that were close to my Pennsylvania home. But New Orleans? My saintly mother said absolutely No! She considered New Orleans the devil's playground! Of course, she had never been there or even close to it. So, I wrote back to the Army telling them I just could not accept that assignment. How naïve I was! I thought that since I had volunteered, I could also refuse. But I soon learned that is not how you respond to official orders. I then received new orders to proceed at once to Camp Forrest in Tennessee, a new camp, way out in the boondocks. It was located between Nashville and Chattanooga, but it might as well have been in the Sahara Desert, as I was to find out.

I was soon on the train, leaving Philadelphia, and family, for the God forsaken town of Tullahoma (such an odd name!), a real one-horse, southern town, including a town square. I have never been further from home than eight miles – to the city where I had had my nurse's training. But I was still determined. This was the beginning of that life I had always wanted. And for that, I could put up with a great deal. And I did. I finally had my opportunity to see my dreams become reality. At this time, the U.S. was still a peaceful country and we would not be actively involved in the war for another seven months when Japan made its attack on Pearl Harbor."

Alice at Camp Forrest in Tennessee

CAMP FORREST, TENNESSEE

May 3, 1943   In the Wild Open Spaces (Tullahoma)

Dear Folks,

If this isn't the pioneer life! And I really and truly like it. It is, what I believe, what I want and I really think that I will be happy here with this outfit. Let me start at the beginning of my adventure, and there are so many things of interest to tell you.

I came over to our site, just a short piece out of Nashville, with Pauline, in a large command car, you know, with curtained sides and sitting high like our old cars used to. So, you really need a ladder to get up into it. After a rough and jolting, yet pleasant ride into our hospital area, I was at my new "station". Our new station is in a large field and consists of thirty large hospital tents, six nurses' tents, office tents, mess tents, mess hall and kitchens, post exchange, Red Cross and supply. It is really a most fascinating set-up. Unless you could really see it, you really would have no idea quite how to picture it. But it is quite a complete unit. The operating room is ideal for a field hospital. They are equipped to run eight operating tables at one time. Although we now have but two set up, for we will be here only about ten days. You see, we are to follow up the various phases of maneuvers. It seems like so much trouble to re-set up the complete unit each time, but such excellent practice and experience for all concerned.

Last night, the surgical service was initiated into the fine art of field surgery as they had an emergency appendectomy at 3 a.m. Everything went very smoothly and the patient even lives to tell the tale! We have about 100 patients with various diagnosis, ranging from measles to appendectomy.

Today, I was really initiated into a soldier's life. I have blisters to prove the point. It is like this. The first thing that all the personnel does on entering an area is to dig an individual "fox hole" which is, as you know, a hole in which to dive in case of an air raid or in case of tank attack. It must be deep enough and wide enough so you can be completely covered so a tank can run over that hole and you can come out unscathed! So, I dug and dug and finally completed it. I wonder if I ever will qualify for professional ditch digger when the war is over!

Now let me tell you about our 'bathroom" and "washroom'. That takes the prize! Our latrine is located about a block down the hill – regulation – and is merely a tent with a three-holer placed over a ditch! Really, quite the thing – ultra – ultra! So, if you get the urge, you treat yourself off down the hill. For washing purposes, we have a huge canvas bag outside our tents for drinking and washing purposes – minor washing, of course. I bought a collapsible canvas wash basin for such purposes and it is indeed a wonderful dollar investment. Today they rigged up hot showers for us a half a mile down the road by a creek. What a treat! And what a luxury! We all felt like new after we had showers, even if they are "open air" and only enclosed on four sides by canvas. The boys have been going down in relays all afternoon, for a shower is such a rare luxury for them.

They have a grand bunch of enlisted men here – they would do anything at all for us and do. And the colonel is an old dear. How grand to have such a wonderful commanding officer. He is always treating us to cokes and giving us all the privileges, he possibly can. He simply cannot do enough for his "girls". We surely do appreciate him. And Pauline is a grand girl too. I lunch in the same tent as she does, since I am to be her assistant.

Our tents are equipped with no electricity, canvas cots and army blankets and a lovely rug of green grass. You know it is quite a change from our inner-spring mattress to a canvas cot, but I can take it, I am for sure no "softy". I awakened early in the morning and found my feet and lower legs extending over the foot of the bed about a foot and a half, so I guess I'll have to elevate the foot of my bed in order to stay in bed! But all in all, I managed to sleep quite well. Luckily, we have had exceptionally lovely weather. Ideal for "camping out". Of course, we do have electricity in all the hospital wards and tents. It's just the nurses' and officers' quarters who do not have it yet. In time, we will though. At present, I am writing by the light of a candle – quite an ingenious thought I had to living here.

Our mess is in a tent out under the sky, as we wish and as weather permits. The food is really good and plentiful, although I have not really been hungry yet. Oh, I eat, but not ravenously as so many are. Our utensils are a tin plate and an enamel soup bowl. From the latter, we partake of coffee, tea or fruit juice. Really, I am sure Emily Post would not approve at all, but we really are roughing it. And the funny part of it is that I am happier here than I was at Forrest. The change is the best thing I could have done, especially now. The cook made the most delicious cakes today – such fine texture and so very tasty, the likes of which you may expect to find in Horn & Hardart's, but really not in an army hospital located in the field!

Can you imagine me going around working in the masculine attire of slacks? Well, that is our uniform here and the only practical one, I assure you. But it does seem funny to go and make ward rounds in slacks. Oh, the tales I shall spin to my nieces and nephews!

We are so close to Nashville, and yet cannot leave the area as that is a maneuver regulation. And I have a shoe ration card I must use before the month is up. I hope I can get to some place where they sell good shoes!

So, come the night and darkness, we turn ourselves into our cozy cots and sleep away the night hours! It sure is a healthy life – fresh air, rest and sunshine. We are the Blue Army and our opposition – the Red Army. If the Red Army capture any of us in their area, they take us as prisoners. So, you see they make it quite realistic. That is the main reason that we are restricted. We wear blue felt armbands as identification.

Well, I guess I have almost exhausted my supply of news and details of my new life. But I do want you to realize I am quite happy and content, and really do believe I will be glad and thankful I have made the change.

All I want to say further, is please write me often, and even if it is only a card. I will appreciate it so much more than ever.

I was quite elated today to return to my tent and find three copies of the Bulletin on my cot. I found out a sergeant here was from Chestnut Hill and he found out I was from Philadelphia and is going to give them to me as he finishes them. Everyone is so thoughtful.

My writing case and clock are sure Godsends now!

Well, I feel right proud of this letter - length- I mean.

Love,   Alice

"I had left behind all the comforts and nicer things of life – and now here I was – in hot and dusty Tennessee. Our home for the next two years was to be a plain wooden barracks, in a new Army post that had just recently been completed. The one redeeming feature was that we each had our own room. Granted, it was not very elegant – in fact, it was very austere – a narrow bed, wooden table and chair, and an open closet for our clothes. But it was our room. I soon learned that there were so many other nurses there in just the same situation. We had all volunteered – as good patriots, and were all here alone – all from northern states. We soon found one another and formed real friendships. No friendships were quite like those formed in the service. We needed one another and we shared so much. It did not take us long to fall into a happy and healthy routine. We were all nurses from many different states and backgrounds, but we had so much in common. And we were happy, for we were all doing just what we had wanted to do for a long time.

Nursing in the Army was vastly different from nursing in civilian life. Our hospital was composed of many long, wooden barracks – connected by long covered walkways. Each ward, or barrack, had thirty-five beds and each was designated according to common diagnosis, i.e., U.R.I., G.I., skin disease, venereal disease, urinary disease, etc. Although there was an RN in charge of each ward, there also was a Ward Master, usually a sergeant, in charge of the ward men who were privates or corporals, and they provided basic patient care and ward duties. Each ward had a Medical Officer in charge of patient care.

It was quite an adjustment for us, not to be giving medications or direct patient care, although we soon did find ways to give patient care. Wasn't that why we were here? The enlisted men were very well trained in caring for patients before they were accepted on the units.

Our patients were often not very ill. They were admitted to the hospital when they were not able to do full duty and they were not discharged until they were ready to return to full duty. So, we had a large convalescent ward.

How young and innocent those enlisted men were! Most had never been away from home before. It was such a joy to be around them. We were all quite happy in our new life. At this time, the U.S. was still a peaceful country and we would not be actively involved in the war for another seven months when Japan made its attack on Pearl Harbor.

Then in the early morning of December 7, 1941, Japan attacked the U.S. Naval Base at Pearl Harbor in Hawaii – destroying almost the entire Pacific fleet. Everything took on a very different meaning, and those innocent, young boys would soon, and quickly, become fighting men, many giving their lives for their country. May God help them.

Now we had no choice. As Germany and Japan were allies, the U.S. finally declared war on both fronts. Suddenly, we were very deeply involved in World War II.

Life went on very pleasantly in spite of the war. But we knew it would never again be the same and that some of us would be leaving for other destinations within the year. At regular periods, notices would be posted for volunteers for overseas assignment. One by one, or often more, our ranks were thinned. Some to Australia, some to the Pacific coast, and a few went home to marry their hometown sweethearts! And then the first notice for the European Theater, and England, were posted. Although I was happy in our safe and secure circle of friends, I knew this was what I had long wanted, so now it was my turn to sign my name. About fifteen of us signed up in July, 1943, and waited anxiously for our orders.

Our orders soon came. We were to form an Evacuation Hospital, and report for the field maneuvers. The rest of that summer was spent on maneuvers in the field. This was simulated warfare, and our first experiences as a hospital unit with our new staff. For some of this time, we were assigned to Ft. Bragg, North Carolina to assist in their maneuvers. This was vastly different from our later experience in Tennessee, for we remained on the post in permanent buildings, and all 'casualties' came to the hospital were set up in one of the barracks. It was a pleasant experience, but certainly did little to prepare us for our life in combat. It was here that our enlisted men found and adopted a brown and white mongrel pup they name Pudgy. She soon became our camp mascot and beloved pet.

As we were to be a mobile tent hospital, similar to a MASH unit, we lived in tents – five to a tent – under the hot Tennessee sun, rain and often mud! Our hospital was totally a tent hospital and we soon knew why we were designated 'Evacuation' hospitals. We received our patients directly from the field of action, having received first aid at the site. Any further surgery would be performed at the hospital and within several days, they would be evacuated by ambulance to a Station or General Hospital. Helicopters had not yet been used for battlefield evacuation. It is not an easy life, but it was the work we wanted to do and we were all happy doing it. There was such satisfaction in it. But there were so many adjustments we had to make.

One of our first responsibilities upon arrival at a new site was to dig – literally – our personal foxhole! It had to be deep enough and wide enough to provide us with complete safety – and that was a lot of digging. On maneuvers, we made about eight moves to new areas, so that meant eight new foxholes! The enlisted men always preceded us to each of our new locations and when we arrived, they had all the tents up, including our 'living-quarters' and that whole process was a big undertaking. I am afraid they were often taken for granted.

Our hospital consisted of thirty large ward tents and our total patient capacity was 450 beds. Our operating rooms were made with four large ward tents – joined to form a cross- and each room was fully equipped – containing three operating tables. We had the potential capacity of twelve O.R. tables, but for maneuvers, we set up only one complete room with three tables. This hospital set up was remarkably complete and amazingly functional. We were soon to find out that we were capable of performing most major procedures done in well-equipped civilian hospitals. The cases were all trauma surgeries, but they were more complex and difficult than most elective surgeries.

If we were fortunate, we would eat our meals in the central 'mess tent', at which time we would enjoy a hot meal of army C-rations. More frequently, we 'feasted' on K-rations. Each box contained one complete meal and they were identified by a large 'B', 'L' or 'D' to indicate breakfast, lunch or dinner. It really made no difference which we selected, for in time, they all tasted the same! They were:

Breakfast – a round tin (size of tuna tin) of ham and eggs, hard tack biscuits (very similar in appearance, consistency and taste to dog biscuits!), jelly and Nescafe powder

Lunch – round tin of cheese (our favorite), biscuits, jelly, a bar of very hard semi-sweet chocolate and lemonade powder

Dinner – round tin of Spam, biscuits, jelly, hard candy and Nescafe powder

In each box, they included toilet paper and several cigarettes, the former always welcome and appreciated. We carried it in the liner of our helmet for ready access!

So, you can understand why hot C-rations (stew, hash, etc.) were always appreciated. We could sit down at a table and eat, even if we did eat out of our metal mess kit, and drink our beverage from our enamel basin! How very welcome were the 'care packages' we received from family and friends! I will elaborate more on these later.

Now a word about our nurse's uniform. It certainly wasn't the nice starched white uniform with cap, white shoes and hose we were used to wearing. No – we wore army fatigues! Not at all feminine or flattering, but so very practical. From this point on, we were indeed 'one of the boys.' We wore leggings that were laced, and into these we tucked our fatigues. We endured these until the day a mobile PX (post exchange) came to our camp and we were all able to purchase paratroop boots. To us they were beautiful and we all discarded our leggings. Our nurse's cap was replaced with a helmet! This kind of life lasted for over two months. Later, looking back on all these experiences, we realized what wonderful preparation it all was for what lay ahead."

Alice gets ready for "maneuvers"

May 27, 1943   Life in the Fields

Dear Folks,

Well, here I am – in another area, having moved here yesterday, quite late in the evening. It was pouring rain when we got
our orders to move into a new area sixty miles away and about sixty
miles from all civilization, too. So, we took down all the tents, packed
everything and set out by convoy to our new home. We arrived late
at night. It had stopped raining and it was surely muddy – as only
Tennessee can be! And the whole unit was set up and made ready to
operate before we hit the day. And it is no easy job for the boys to put up
about 50 tents in the mud and dark, but it was done. It was dark when
we arrived here, so it wasn't until this morning, that we really saw the
surrounding countryside and what a beautiful location we have here.
High, heavily wooded hills on all sides. Flowers and grass make our
floors for our tents. And all day long, the wind blows just enough to
keep it nice and pleasantly cool for us. It apparently was the home of
cows before we intruded, for at sites, they left many calling cards and

we must be careful of our footing! I cannot quite understand it, but there are so much flowering citrus plants around here. I was always under the impression that they were found in dry, sandy areas.

So far, neither of my two tents have patients. How anyone could find us to bring patients is beyond me, for we came through miles of little dirt roads. And even at our place, we had to run through a deep creek, which was flowing across the road. It really is remarkable what these army vehicles can do!

Before my dinner, I dug my foxhole, by choice, for I feel we should dig our own. Why should the nurses be here to make more work for the boys, for they have plenty to do if they do their own work? It is a hot, dirty job, but I did it and took a "bird bath" afterwards. It is really remarkable how refreshed you can feel after such a bath! Cold water, too! It would be such a luxury to sit in a tub full of hot, soapy water!

I had a letter from Johnny last night. He seems quite happy and so much older and more sensible for his years than he was when he was last home. If we return to Camp Gordon, I will be about 250 miles from Johnny, so perhaps I will be able to get a few days off and go and see him. A few days leave wouldn't take me home, as it is quite a distance from here, so you see how it would be. Time alone will tell. But I surely would love to see Johnny, for I believe it would help him too, for naturally he is homesick to a certain extent, although it can't be detected by his letters.

I guess I'll close now and write soon again. I wrote Johnny and Aunt Julia today, so I feel I've done my share and deserve a rest. Keep on writing   – Love Alice

June 2, 1943   Somewhere in Tennessee

Dear Folks,

Just a scribbled note while we are again waiting for transportation and orders to move. Half of our equipment and personnel has already gone on ahead to our new camp, which is about 25 miles from this spot. We got our orders to move early this morning, as the "blue army", our opposing force, is closing in on our area and we have to pull out, patients and all – except, of course, our very sick patients, as soon as is humanly possible. For our protection, some infantry troops were sent to our area here to guard us against any opposing attackers! They surely do make the maneuvers as realistic as possible. But the boys are now becoming quite disgusted and tired of moving so frequently. This is our fifth complete move in less than a month, and each time they have to dig foxholes and then fill them up before they leave again. So, their morale is quite low right now, and I can't blame them. We have a healthy bunch of officers and yet the enlisted men have to put up the officers' tents, dig them foxholes, and pull down their tents and fill up their foxholes and do all their own work after that! This is all very wrong and contrary to army regulations. If the men do this work for the officers, they are supposed to be paid for it by them. But not these fellows! They sit around and play ball while the men work and do not offer them a cent. Naturally their morale is going to be low! What else could you expect? Doctors surely do not, as a common rule, make very good army officers. And naturally, the boys have all been restricted to the area as we have been. I only hope they will be given furloughs when maneuvers are over.

Another thing, in any outfit, the enlisted men are supposed to be fed first and then the officers. But not with our officers. They will break through the chow line all the time and kick if an enlisted man fares better than he does. I sure hate to see that and say that, but it is so. They really need a regular army man to head the outfit and right a few wrongs and all would be fine and dandy – for they really have a good outfit here. Perhaps in time, things will be different.

It is really funny – the boys have termed this outfit "Col. R's Traveling Medicine Show". Remember the old medicine shows that traveled around the country? Really quite appropriate!

No one told me a thing about the fire at the Platinum Works and I read about it last night in an old Bulletin on the front page. Come, come. And I also read that Catherine King is in Africa with Eisenhower's staff.

3:00 P.M.

Still waiting for orders and transportation to leave for our new site. It is quite a problem, for we have not had our quota of transporting vehicles issued to us. Some of us, while we are waiting, we went up the lane to a little store and got a coke and one of life's rare luxuries – a popsicle! They sell them once a week here and today happened to be the day for it – lucky day for us! But we hate to leave our little creek and big shade trees and nice breeze. I understand that the area we are to go to next is lacking in shade and I am sure we will have no creek. Such good fortune could not be ours twice in succession! It is the understanding, I believe, that on this move, we are to learn the fine art of camouflage. It really should be quite interesting.

Julia, surely by this date, you have heard from the Navy again as to the date of your assignment to duty. And I would not get many uniforms, for I believe the Navy is quite prompt in supplying such articles. I can think of nothing to remind you to get to take along, for as far as I know, most Navy stations are situated near towns or cities, and you will live quite a civilized life in comparison to we in the army.

4:00 P.M.

Well, transportation finally arrived and here I sit, in the front of a big army truck, on our way! I doubt if there is any vehicle aside from a tank, which I have not ridden in!

We're off! Good day –

Love to all, Alice

CAMP GORDON, GEORGIA – DECISION TO GO OVERSEAS

July 22, 1943

Dear Julia,

Again, I pen you a few lines – and hot and tired as I am, I know it will be worth the effort I put forth, for I realize fully just what it will mean to you. There is not a breath of air here in my room and I am slowly melting away. I guess it is fairly cool where you are, being so close to the water. I do hope you are happy there, Julia, and I am very anxious to hear from you and hear all about your work and life, and just everything – so do not keep me waiting, please.

I had quite a long talk with Pauline today, after she had been talking to our new commanding officer. Who, by the way, is going to be okay. He really is getting our men, including our wonderful officers, to work making crates and packing instruments and supplies. And if he could do that, he has the right stuff in him! He is all for getting things for us and looking out for our welfare.

And then she asked me at noon today, if I would take over the operating room as supervisor, instead of being her assistant – for she feels I am most suited for the O.R., more so than any of the other girls. Not trying to repeat praise, just facts and for you, only I tell it. Well, you can realize how I felt. For the O.R. is the biggest and most important place in an evacuation hospital, and especially overseas! I have not been in an O.R. since my second year in training, so I am green! But I am willing to try. So, tomorrow, I go to this O.R. to work and learn the Army way. I sure am scared – they have thirty operations scheduled and if they ask me to scrub, I'll pass out! I only wish I had a little confidence in myself! Pauline told the Chief Nurse here, Major Galli, so she would put me in the O.R. to work. Major said that *she had made an excellent choice and would not be sorry! I was dumb-founded when she said this, for I did not even know the old girl knew my name! Then Pauline told me Major Reilly, our executive officer, told her she could not have done a wiser thing or made a better change! Now, why can't I have a little confidence in my own ability? Then too, this will mean I will receive my First Lieutenant's rating, if all goes well. I would have gotten it as her assistant too, but really, I will like this job better, I hope. Keep your fingers crossed for me and please say nothing at home. I want to be certain beyond doubt first, before any-thing is said. Please do this for me.*

I must retire and don't let yourself get down, Julia. There is too much to be up about! Write soon –

Good night!

Love, Al

"We finally got our orders, after the completion of Tennessee maneuvers in late summer of 1943, to report to Camp Gordon, Georgia, which was near Augusta. Here we were to prepare our unit and ourselves for our overseas assignment. I was not able to make the trip with our unit as I had been very ill with Shigella dysentery. The symptoms came on very suddenly while I was visiting dear friends at Camp Forrest. It seems our cook was a carrier! I had come to the camp to say goodbye, and spent two weeks in the hospital, with all the usual symptoms. The chief Nurse of Camp Forrest, Major Moat, and her assistant, Captain Goldie Abel (who had been a dear friend for the two years I had spent at Camp Forrest) were wonderful to me! I was so fortunate to have been there when I was ill, instead of enroute by truck convoy all the way to Georgia.

I joined my own outfit in Georgia, making the trip by Pullman train and missing that long ride by truck. We spent about two and a half months at Camp Gordon, receiving further training and making prepa-rations for our overseas assignment. It had been the original plan that I was to be assistant chief nurse in our hospital and I felt quite good about that. Then I was asked to accept the position of Operating Room supervisor, the plum of all the nursing positions! I was very flattered and too naïve to even question this appointment. I had always enjoyed my O.R. and Emergency Room assignments, but I realized that I had had no advanced training or extensive experience in the operating room. Yet I reasoned to myself – why not? I had learned early in my army experience, never refuse or question such decisions. Remember New Orleans? I felt as qualified, or more so, as any of the other nurses. I was greatly encouraged when the Chief Nurse of Camp Gordon told me she thought I was an excellent choice, and several of our own medical officers told me I was the best one for that position. Looking back now, I do wonder why I ever felt qualified for the huge job and responsibility. Yet for someone who had wanted for so long to be an Army nurse, I knew that this was the type of nursing I had always visualized. So, this great responsibility on my young shoulders – I was only 24 years old, we finally received orders to report to Fort Dix, New Jersey, for our overseas assignment. All under the cloak of secrecy. This was at last, what we all had been preparing for."

August 3, 1943

Dear Mother,

Thank you so much for your very sweet letter that I just received. If you could only realize how very much it means to me for you to take such a beautiful attitude. I fully realize that it is hard for you. It isn't exactly easy for me when I really think of all it will mean, but I do know. I know this as I have never known anything before, that it is what I want and just what I should do. I can't explain the feeling I have, but in my mind, there is no questions or doubts. And then to have such a beautiful letter from you and to have you so wisely understand. I feel that I am doing what is right. One is satisfied to stay here and do their share for a while. But after a certain time, you feel that you are needed more in another part of this world, where we can really do a more important job. And Mother, you do not, and

24

WAITING ON ORDERS TO GO OVERSEAS

September 25, 1943   1:15 A.M.

Dearest Julia,

Sitting here in the early morning listening to lovely organ music, interspersed with lovely sentimental poems. Makes me feel sad for some reason. Off and on all day, I have felt that way. Tonight, I heard Helen MacGregor sing "America the Beautiful" and I could have easily wept. Somehow, listening to her and hearing the beautiful words of the song, made me feel our land was indeed worth fighting for! And then, I'll think of the folks and home, and I realize how very long it will be! I want to go – it is my choice, but it isn't easy, as you must know. Julia, when I think of all you and I have been to one another, how close we always were, I just cannot picture not seeing or speaking with you for so long a period of time. It does not seem right or possible. Yet within a few days, it is going to be a start of that long separation anyway. You may have many a time, thought I was hard and unfeeling to leave home and all of you for camp, but I assure you, there were times when I was so lonely and unhappy, I did not feel I could stand it. Last Christmas was the worst time of all. What will this Christmas be! I pray we are so busy we will not have time to think of it!

I should not be writing this to you, but I had to talk with someone. You'll never know the mixture of emotions within me as we are preparing to leave. Part of me wants to go so badly, but part just clings to all that stands for home.

Today we were issued our mattress covers to use at P.O.E., for the nurse turnover is so rapid, they do not use sheets and this way is more sanitary.

I am still waiting for your picture – hurry up sister! And if you never do another thing for me on this earth, please write me often when I leave. I am depending on you, Julia.

I'll write again tomorrow – this isn't a letter, just a few thoughts and feelings on paper.

Love Always, Al

November 6, 1943   Camp Gordon.

Dear Julia,

I guess this is to be my farewell letter from Camp Gordon. For when this reaches you, I shall be at the P.O.E. – yet until I get on the train, I refuse to believe it. I really do not think it has fully dawned on me that it is all so. Instead, it seems like a dream and won't materialize. Perhaps one day, you shall know just what I am attempting to say. I wrote Mother the day before yesterday and told her. She has been good about everything so far. It makes it so much easier for me that she can take it as she has. I guess you got my letter asking you about the Christmas gifts. I was in town yesterday and bought a nice compact for Goldie, so you can cross her name off the list. So that will be one less for you to have to bother about.

I wish you could see me all rigged up – gas mask, pistol belt, helmet, canteen, and musette bag! I took several pictures this morning and that completed the film I used on my leave, which were those we took of you – remember? I am sending them home to be developed as I have no time here and Mother can send them over to me. I would like to see them all.

Julia, do write often to me – even a card will do. But I am going to be awfully lonesome as you can imagine – so I shall depend on you a bit to stick by me. And you can be sure I shall write you just as often as I can.

Be good Julia, think of me once in a while and I shall likewise think of you. Don't worry about me – no matter what may come to pass. For I am not depending one whit on my own power to keep me safe, but I have put my trust in God, who is able to keep us all. Julia, if I had no belief or faith, I just could not go. How the others are doing it is beyond me!

I shall not say goodbye, just au revoir and I'll write again as soon as I am allowed. My new A.P.O. will be sent out today.

God bless you – be good and keep the home fires burning.

Love always, Al

FORT DIX, NEW JERSEY -
DEPLOYMENT - ENROUTE

"In November, 1943, we were in Ft. Dix, on our way, but still not sure where we would be going. Everything was hush hush, but somehow, we all knew it would be to the European Theater of Operations (E.T.O.). That was where we all wanted to go, for that was where all the activity seemed to be concentrated. And we realized the Allies were planning an invasion of Europe. We were kept so busy with our 'shots', instructions and last-minute supplies, that our week at Ft. Dix passed very quickly. We received our final orders to leave for New York harbor to board our ship and head for Europe.

Finally, we were on our way, and by now we knew that our destination had to be England. Where else could we be headed? We would soon find out for certain. As England was my father's birthplace, I was looking forward to seeing his homeland.

We were sailing on the 'Aquitania', a British liner of the Cunard Line. The remarkable fact was it was on this very ship that my parents sailed on their honeymoon to England in 1914, just prior to the outbreak of World War I in Europe. It was still a fine ship, stripped as it was of most of the elegant furnishings, as it now was in full service as a troop ship for the United States.

The Aquitania had been requisitioned by the British government. They left New York Harbor on November 17, 1943. They were 39 officers, one warrant officer, 48 nurses and 248 enlisted men.

Our 'stateroom' was meant to accommodate two people, but was now home for nine nurses for the next week. There were triple decker beds, and very little room for anything else. I was assigned top bunk. One had to be part monkey to reach it and then climb back down. But I was very young and agile then! However, between nerves and the motion of the ship, most of us were seasick at least part of the next few days. No Dramamine in those days for us! Under those conditions, that can present a real problem. But we all did survive.

One bright spot was the dining room. The ship was staffed with a British crew, so in the dining room, we were all treated to the finer aspects of British dining, such as five course dinners! When we were physically able to go down to it, it was such a welcome break from military meals. Of course, this was only for the officers. The enlisted men had their usual mess hall elsewhere. It really could not be any other way, as the ship carried a very large number of troops. Our unit was a very small part of the passenger list.

We were quite restricted on board, but there were large lounges for our use. At certain daytime periods, we were allowed up on deck. What a vast, lonely span of angry gray water! It did not take us very long to realize we were alone on that big sea, as we were not part of a convoy. This was not very reassuring, for usually troop ships traveled in large convoys with escorts, but we were alone. We were also aware that German U-boats (submarines) did frequently travel these sea lanes. We had several scares, but we did arrive at our destination safely. God had to have been watching over us. Quite an experience."

November 19, 1943   Enroute.

Evening

Dearest Julia,

I am right proud of myself, for despite the fact that there is so very little to write about, due to censorship regulations, I have already, today, written three letters and a similar number yesterday. Really not a bad number, I should say. So here is one for you. I wrote you an air-mail – V. mail, yesterday morning and I am anxious to know which one reaches you first. When you write me next time, do let me know which one you receive first. And that is how I shall write after this.

This is really a very pleasant trip and we are all enjoying it, despite crowded conditions. In fact, it is quite difficult to realize that there is a war and that this is not a pleasure trip. For at present, I am in the officers' lounge. Cards and music are the main sources of amusement here.

You know, it is a funny thing to go to bed at night and not know what may happen and yet sleep like a baby all night! I have no fear myself, but if I were the majority of our folks, I sure would. They are the most self-satisfied group. I guess there is not half a dozen God-fearing ones in the group. Why, they proudly state they are heathens! If I did not know for a certainty, Julia, that God was with me and over my every move all the time, I would be most afraid and unhappy. It is such a comfort to really know that unless He so wills it, no harm can come my way. And if it does, I will have life eternal. I am not writing just words. I realize, more than ever since I have undertaken this job, how very important it is to have Christ as your own Savior. A few years ago, I would not have written this, although I knew it, but feel it should be talked about now. I only feel badly that I have gone so long, saying so little.

I just wish you were here with me to make this trip with me and to be with me throughout all that shall come about. Why didn't you join up when I did!

I am happy and although I miss all of you so much, think of what a grand reunion it shall someday be! May God speed up that day!

Do write real soon and real often to me.

Love always Al

OUR ARRIVAL IN GREAT BRITAIN

"We arrived during the night and docked in the Firth of Clyde in Scotland. When we awakened in the early morning, we realized we were no longer in motion. When we looked out our porthole – what a picture! Green hills and a lovely quaint village on the waterfront. And terra firma, once again, would soon be under our feet.

On to the British train to take us to our destination in England. We made the overnight trip through Scotland and England, finally arriving at our destination – the small village of Wotten-Under-Edge. Such unusual names they had for their quaint little villages!"

November 25, 1943
Thanksgiving Day   Somewhere in England
Dear Mother and All,

Thanksgiving Day and perhaps you folks at home feel that I have nothing to be thankful for. But today is a true Thanksgiving Day for me. I have so very many, many things for which I should and am thankful. There is so much I want to write you, I hardly know just where to start, so perhaps I should just start.

First and foremost, we had a safe and lovely trip over. Our last two days were quite rough, in fact very rough, but we came through. I guess I am not a very good Sailor, for I sure was seasick for four days. So, after my return trip, I shall venture forth as a sailor no more. I can assure you! All in all, though, we did have a nice trip. When I come home, I shall tell you more of it, as it is now, we can say nothing of it as to name of boat and route. Never was I so glad to see land! We docked at dark and did not see a thing until daylight. What a beautiful sight! One of the girls remarked, "Why is all in technicolor?", and how descriptive that was! Beautiful hills and lovely quaint villages on the waterfront. How I wish Aunt Ann had been there to see it!

We then had quite a train trip and I love the British trains! They are so comfortable – their little compartments so comfortable, too. How wonderfully everything had been planned for us! Red Cross waiting with coffee and doughnuts at port and again with supper at another spot. They are doing one grand job!

Today we arrived and I wish Dad was there to know I am here. How thrilled he would be. And what beautiful countryside they have here! It is hard to realize there is a war, just to see the peaceful scenes of sheep grazing on the hillsides and green grass and hawthorn. It is so hard to try to describe the place, but you know what it is like, Mother, having been here abouts.

Now, let me tell you about our present circumstances. We are in this lovely and quaint old town. I cannot tell you the name and all of the nurses and officers are being "billeted" at various homes. Some, one to a home, other four to one home. We are three to a home. We are in a lovely, old English home – formerly a nursing home run by two elderly women – old – and yet with every modern convenience you could desire. Hawthorn grows all over the house. And the English ivy, the first I have ever seen since I left home. It is so picturesque! These two women are lovely – so hospitable and sweet. They have also, a refugee from Hampstead and she lives here. I have a lovely little room to myself – so cozy and comfortable and the other two girls have a room together – equally as attractive. The ladies gave us each an old-fashioned foot warmer or hot water bottle. Call it what you may, it feels so good! For it is quite cold here now. Then, a little later, they brought us each a steaming cup of Bovril, which was so tasty. Really hit the spot! So, after a hot bath and clean clothing, I crawled into my bed with my foot warmer to write home. I guess that brings me up to date.

So, you can see, we are being treated royally and really almost spoiled! I am sure you will feel better after you receive this letter. That is why I am trying to get it out to you as soon as possible instead of sleeping.

And shortly, we depart to our common mess hall to partake of our Thanksgiving Dinner of pork, having arrived too late for turkey. But we had turkey last week on the boat, so we do not feel neglected.

I do want you to send this on to Julia. I am going to write to her after dinner, but not all this detail.

I wish I could write more details for you, but you do understand, I know.

It will be so wonderful to hear from you. I have had no mail for so long. None of us have, of course. It will all come in a pile – make mine a big one please!

So, you see, I have so many things to thank God for, and I do, and do not worry about me. I am well fixed.

I do hope all is well at home and take care of yourself for me. God bless all of you.

Nurses' quarters in Wotton-Under-Edge

View from Alice's window in Wotten-Under-Edge

WOTTEN-UNDER-EDGE

"We were soon to learn how and where we were all to live for the next few months (as it turned out, we were there for seven months) until plans were finalized for the invasion. We were not thinking of that at the time. We were too excited and anxious to learn where we were going now. We had the plan explained to us and it was a good one. All the nurses and other officer (MD's and executive staff) were to be in private homes, which our government had arranged to use for as long as needed. The home owners were well reimbursed, but it must have created a great inconvenience in their family life. This arrangement was called 'billeting'. We were to live in these homes, but all our meals and social times, and preparations, were to be in our central Mess Hall and meeting room in the area. There were three to four nurses assigned to each home, depending on the size of the home.

Personnel spent most of their time getting their hospital ready-sorting and organizing instruments. These were the days before plastics and disposables. And penicillin had just been introduced in hospitals. Everything was reusable and had to be sterilized. There were no disposable I.V., blood sets, drapes, gloves, masks, needles, syringes or basin – none of those things you take for granted. We had our own autoclave that kept our supplies sterile. And it never failed us.

All our wrappers and surgical drapes had to be made by our staff – and sewn on sewing machines that today (1993) would be found in a museum! We had no electric machines and most were not even treadle operated. Most of them had to be sewn by one person while another turned the wheel that made it run. To make the job even more complex, all our O.R. tents had to have complete liners – made of sheeting – to assure cleanliness, for that part of the tent was directly over the field of operation. Canvas tents that are put up and taken down so frequently in all kinds of weather and terrain are not very sanitary. Our hospitals were dismantled and set up as frequently as every 7-10 days. As the army front advanced, so did evacuation hospitals. In addition to the cleanliness, the clean white linen certainly added much to the brightness of the room. We literally sewed miles making these four huge linings."

November 25, 1943
Thanksgiving Day
Dearest Julia,

Somewhere in England

Thanksgiving Day – and look where I am! It is the oddest thing to really try and realize that I am not in the United States any longer, but that I have crossed the ocean and am in England! That is the way we felt on the trip across, too. As if we were just going to another camp on the continent. Sort of like living a dream and not expecting it to materialize at all! But the very obvious fact remains so, for here I sit in a lovely home in England – not too far from London and we are going to have tea with the couple of elderly ladies who own the place! Really, Julia, this is an experience, from start to finish, that I would not have missed for a thing! Of course, so far, this has seemed like a pleasure trip than any other thing. But our time of work and hardship will come too soon, I guess. So, we are making the most of the present, as is to be expected.

I wrote a long letter to Mother this noon and asked her to send it to you. It has more detail, so I won't have to repeat myself too much. I will explain a few things to you, however.

All of the nurses and officers are "billeted out" in private home as we have no other living facilities here for us. There are three of us here in this lovely old English home, with three lovely elderly women. Two of them were nurses and they formerly ran a nursing home here. They have been so very sweet to us since we came this morning. They just make you feel at home and go out of their way to do nice little odds and ends for you, such as tea now. What a nice tea it was! Currant jam on biscuits and real tea! What a treat after all our pseudo coffee! It is so odd to see a town come completely "blacked out" and naturally, that is how things are here. And they do it religiously, too.

I was just thinking that if only you had been in our outfit and with me! Wouldn't it be just wonderful! But as is, I do not have anyone I can call a real friend, as I have always had since I have been in the Army. But I am biding my time. I want a real friend again this time.

I have been inquiring here about Doris and if we have sufficient time free, I will try to go to see her. I think it would be nice.

Everything has turned out so nicely and run so smoothly so far. I could ask for nothing except a safe return home, not too far in the future. I have so much to be truly thankful for, and I am. I thank God for all of it, especially our safe voyage. We were so fortunate.

I guess I'll receive all my mail in a pile. Please write often and V-mail comes in 9 days. I guess air mail is quicker. Write long letters though.

Much love to you dear, Alice

"We soon settled into a routine way of life – exploring our quaint new area. We took long walks – five to eight miles, to get exercise we needed and to enjoy such a lovely and very different part of our world.

Our brightest spot in any day – or week or later every month – was mail call. How welcome each piece of mail was. This was our link to home and friends. Due to the sporadic "schedule" and great uncertainty of delivery, our mail usually arrived in great bundles. I was very fortunate and always received a lot of mail. I had such a faithful family and dear friends. I was very consistent in writing long letters daily as the situation permitted. And how we looked forward to packages from home we termed "care" packages. And that is just what they were. Especially when we were in the field and later in combat - they were our lifeline. These packages from home contained packaged soups, jellies, candy, toiletries, gum, fruit cakes, magazines, warm socks and even long underwear!

Every package was a surprise ad we all shared in these goodies. Many a cold winter night, we enjoyed chicken noodle soup in our tents heated on top of our pot-bellied stove.

We found life in rural England very pleasant. Our host family was so kind and so thoughtful and we were treated as guests. They made our life as home-like as possible.

The countryside was so beautiful — rolling hills, beautiful gardens, quaint old homes. Every home, no matter how unpretentious, had an old wall encasing it and each home had a name. Hawthorne trees abounded and the cry of the mockingbird was new to us. The roses were so large, even those climbing up the side of the home, and every home had roses in abundance. Life here was at a much slower pace, and the people seemed to dwell so much in the past history of the country — and there was history in everything and every place. It was no wonder their poetry was so beautiful and the literary masterpieces have lived on through many centuries. They have the time and inspiration.

I have said nothing so far about the blackouts. We were initiated on the trip over as the ship had to observe total blackout. Here in England, for the local people it was a way of life. For us, it was a radical change. No light of any kind was to be seen from outside. Every window and door had a black curtain that was drawn closed as soon as time came for indoor lights to be on. The most difficult part to adjust to was the total darkness outside, for no light of any kind was allowed to show through the windows or doors. There were special civilian wardens appointed to patrol for any infractions. Most nights, you could not see your hand in front of your face!"

November 27, 1943   Somewhere in England

Dear Mother and All,

I find I shall have to write a joint family letter. It seems to work out better than an individual one. I do hope you can understand that is the only reason. I will try to write you every day, as long as I can. I hope I do not bore you with my daily record of events.

Today is a typical English day I am told – drizzly and cold and foggy. Up until today, we have had sunny and crispy cold days, quite cheerful. Today you can think only of spending it in front of a roaring fire if you could find such a fire! How the English can stand such cold homes is beyond me. Of course, I do realize that part of it is due to fuel shortages, but not all of it. They appear quite content in a beastly cold room! We are finding that difficult to get used to. And some of the homes have no hot water for bathing or washing! Why, the average American lives in real luxury in comparison to a lot of these well-fixed English families. But they are so quaint. So slow and dreamy and live so in the past. It is easy to see why such beautiful poetry and masterpieces came from the English – they have the inspiration and the time. There is not the hustle and hurry here as we have it. And the land is so pretty. Nature is so soft here. And everything is so green and colorful. Even beautiful rose gardens are out – still in bloom.

Last night, a group of us nurses and officers, went to a town carnival – like we used to have and had the time of our lives – second childhood. Then we took a lovely walk in the blackout and then had to walk one another home! We went to one home – really an old manor house, where one old lady and her maid live – a huge place full of antiques. That is one thing about most of the homes here. They are full of things any antique lover would give so much to possess. Beautiful old dishes and furniture and brass and copper pieces. There is real beauty over here. I spent the night with one of the girls who lived alone and didn't like it! The place was very gloomy and every board creaked and groaned and she was frightened, so I stayed. We were hearing queer noises all night!

It is so odd to walk in the street at night, for they naturally have total blackouts here. And I do mean total. Looking down from a hill last night, you would never have known that there was a house there, let alone a town! They really are very religious about their blackouts.

When we first came, we gave all the town children candy and gum, for they are rationed "sweets" and rarely get it. But we soon learned that that was the wrong thing to do! Now – they see you coming and run to meet you saying "Any candy please?" They are regular little beggars!

I am having quite a time with this new money system of England. I just have to trust them – handing them a coin and trusting I get the correct change in return! But they are quite honest. Although I do say, and always shall, that I much prefer our American money system. It is much simpler all around!

Guess where I went last night? In a pub! Of all places! I just had to see what one was like and I did! But I didn't order ale. I ordered cider. And if ever you wish a good, strong laxative, this will fill the bill! I guess this will do for the day and as soon as we get settled and organized, I guess I will write much less, so I'll spare you while I can.

Mother, I do hope you are staying well and taking it easy. And I hope all the others are well too.

Much love and do write soon and often.

Love always, Alice

November 31, 1943   Somewhere in England

Wednesday evening
Dear Mother, Ernie, Fran and Ed,

I guess to date, my letters home had seemed very self-centered and thinking back over them, I do realize that I must have seemed to you to be disinterested in all of you and your welfare. Far, far from that! I am now more interested in that than before. For I cannot now keep in very close contact, so it naturally concerns me more. I do hope you will keep me informed of any such goings on. I want to know how all of you are doing and what concerns you, also concerns me, I assure you. So do keep me posted on that.

I am afraid I am as bad as these English folks when it comes to "tea". Here I sit at 4 P.M. hoping for a cup of tea! And if any of us are out in town at tea-time, we sort of naturally drop into a little bakery store and have a "spot of tea" and two-penny's worth of sweet rolls! Oh, by the time I leave here, you shall have a full-fashioned English child! And I am also catching onto your crazy monetary system here. It is all in getting used to it.

8:00 P.M.

Our kind ladies fixed up a nice little room downstairs for our use in the evenings. It has a nice little fireplace in it and some comfortable chairs and we have it quite to ourselves here, so it is very nice and homey. They do all they possibly can to make us feel "at home". I do hope, and imagine now we will be here for Christmas. It will make it so much easier to be here in a nice home and have a nice fire, instead of a cold tent in the middle of nowhere! You see, I am still quite sentimental about Christmas!

Today – no mail again! All that comes is V-mail and I guess you are not writing that way. It may be a good idea to write V-mail once in a while, for it does come more quickly.

Well, keep writing and keep well.

Love to all of you, Alice

December 3, 1943   Somewhere in England

Dearest Folks,

A typical English day - foggy, cold and quite dismal indeed! And still no mail from the States!

Today, we went on a five-mile hike - all the nurses. It was not a nice day and the fog was quite heavy and it was cold, but still we went. My, but the country is lovely here! The homes are so old and yet none of them have that appearance of neglect or shabbiness. They are quite picturesque instead. The old walls around almost every home is covered with heavy ivy or other vines, and really it all makes such a lovely picture. Ivy grows here like honeysuckle at home! It is cold and we have frost, yet everything remains green. I picked a beautiful bunch of green holly - the prettiest I ever saw, and mistletoe, too! Really in season here!

But the children are so lovely here! The little red, red cheeks and they dress them more colorfully here - yellow, green, orange or blue outfits. They really are adorable and so much healthier than our kids at home appear.

Well, do keep writing. I shall, someday, have quite a pile of mail!

I trust all is well at home and take care of yourself, Mother.

Love to all, Alice

December 7, 1943   Somewhere in England

Dearest Mother,

It was so good to hear from you yesterday - our first real mail from the states! But I must put you straight about this censorship affair. Your letters coming over here are not subject to censorship. It is our mail going to you that is censored. So, don't hesitate to write me as you please. And do not let fear of anyone else reading personal mail make your letter stiff and stinted.

And do keep on writing, for I really expected more than one letter from both Fran and you. But of course, by the time you get this,

I know I shall have received more. In fact, I guess it will be quite close to Christmas at the time you finally receive this. If so, I want you all to have a grand Christmas Day. Think of me and know I would love to be with you if I could, but do not worry about me at all. I am well and too well cared for! Just have one of our good old Christmas days and sing a few carols for me.

Today we all took a five-mile hike – all uphill and quite rapid, and as a result, we are all exhausted tonight. Some of our officers forget we are not men and out do it. But Miss McLin has been told of it and I know she will put an end to it at once. She is all for us and so very fair and square. I like her and do admire her so much. Anyway, four of us stayed at the tail end and thumbed one of the army trucks – riding home the last two miles! And still, we too are so tired tonight.

Sunday, a group of us went into Bath – to see the city and the ancient Roman baths and Bath Abbey – a lovely old cathedral built in 1300. The baths are an excavation and date back almost two thousand years. Also, you know, Bath was quite blitzed about a year ago and we saw evidence of it.

I hope you are taking it a little easier Mother, now that winter is here and take care of yourself. Let me know what you get Julia for Christmas from me.

Love to all of you always, Alice

December 9, 1943   Somewhere in England

Dear Mother and All,

More mail again from home yesterday – eight more letters – from Fran, you, Ed, Julia, Peg and Miss Reilly. It is such a treat to get mail once more. And awful for those who are not so fortunate! I have written home almost every day, including while on the ship, and although our out-going mail is held up for fifteen days after we land, you will receive it all in one group. So, you should receive at least a dozen letters from me when you finally do get them. From now on, our mail will go straight to the states after passing the censor. So, you will not have too long to wait. I will either send them air mail or V-mail, unless I cannot do otherwise. I guess that covers that subject fully.

Last night a convoy of us went to see the operetta "The Gondoliers" given in a neighboring town. It was quite cleverly done by amateurs and we did all enjoy it. It is quite remarkable how good our outfit has done in seeing that we are able to see the various plays and towns around and dances for those who are so inclined.

I did tell you, I believe, that I wrote cousin Doris inviting myself to a visit. And today I received the sweetest letter from her. I will quote part of it, for I thought it very sweet of her – "I am so glad you intend to pay us a visit. I will come and meet you, if possible, if you can let me know the time and station. Perhaps you had better send a telegram. I guess your mother told you she was over here at the outbreak of the other war in 1914 and what fun we had together! I still cannot believe that your father has gone. He was greatly loved here and we still laugh at some of the things he used to say and do. It was lovely of you to write and you are certainly welcome here and to stay and do as you would at home. My love to your mother when you write and the same to yourself, Alice. – Cousin Doris". Now wasn't that a sweet invitation? I shall go to see her on my three-day leave. I do not know just when I can get my three-day pass, but as soon as I know, I will write her and tell her.

Now, how are you doing yourself? How is your blood pressure now? Or don't you bother to check on it? Do take care of yourself and take it easy. And all of the rest of you home folks – take care of yourself – Ernie, Frances and Eddie. And do write often and remember – all details are of interest to me and your letters are not censured.

Much love to all, Alice

December 12, 1943   Somewhere in England

Dearest Mother,

Well, yesterday, I spent in London, being there on a 24-hour pass, which I shall have in addition to my three-day leave. Churchie and I went together leaving the evening before. Our three-day leave we shall spend New Year's Eve in London! And on New Year's Day, there is a choral service at Westminster Abbey, which we shall be able to attend. That will be very impressive, I am sure. Well, we stayed at the Red Cross in London. For three shilling a night, they provide very clean, comfortable quarters in Lester Square – I should say Berkley Square, very close to Piccadilly. So, it is quite central for us.

We started out at nine the next morning – for we were tired when we arrived, for we had to stand almost all of the 100 miles to London on first class tickets! We got a taxi and four of us saw the main spots of London, ending our tour at Buckingham Palace in time to see them changing guards – which is quite a ceremony – if you ever saw it during peacetime. Then they were in full dress uniform. Now they wear just regular uniforms.

We stopped on our tour to see St. Paul's Cathedral. It is a lovely old structure. I remember you saw it on your honeymoon. It is still lovely, although it has, too, been through the blitz. We got there just as the bells were ringing. They rang for a full fifteen minutes. I do not know the occasion, but it was beautiful.

Then we saw Westminster Abbey. It, too, has seen the blitz. It seems that a very large percentage of the churches, no matter how small, have been made targets. Some are merely shells of a church. Westminster was lovely. I shall go back and see it again when I have my leave. We saw the Tower and the Bridge, but not very close, as we had to hurry to see the change of guards.

But London is not at all what it used to be, so all the people tell you. It has seen a lot and taken so much and still the people are so good to you – doing all they can in a very cheerful manner.

The city is full of the old cabs – quite quaint, they are! And it is so easy to see the difference in the "Bobbies" here and our police at home. Everyone looks up to them and respects them for themselves and not their positions. They really are someone over here.

We wanted to be quite swanky, so we went to the Ritz Hotel for dinner and it really is "ritzy".! A lovely room and a lovely table. So, they send us a menu – all written in French! So, what do we do? Ask our waiter to translate, of course! So, we ordered Guinea hen. It seems you have no choice after that. It all goes with it! So, we had sprouts and new potatoes and cake with rum sauce and had the vilest coffee I ever had! And that is all – no salad or anything else and a cost of one pound for two of us! Next time, I eat in the nicest little café I can find. I never liked being ritzy anyway!

Of all songs, they are now playing "White Christmas"! Reminds me – we had some lovely snow yesterday in London. Large flakes and it snowed for almost ten minutes! Then sleeted, then rained, then the sun came out! But at least we had none of the famous fog! At night, we had a beautiful full moon.

How I would love a big dish of ice cream! Or a piece of choco-late candy, or a piece of sweet cake or cookies! Pig, yes. But if ever you feel like sending me something, that is what I'd love, for we cannot get that over here, unless you have coupons. And, of course, we have none. I tried to buy a lovely handkerchief – linen from Robinson and Cleavers. Isn't that a familiar name to you? It seems I heard it before and I needed coupons for it!

Well, I must write Julia. Do take care of yourself and write me often – all of you.

Love to all, Alice

I saw some lovely thatched roof cottages – so picturesque. I didn't know they still had them, but they are so quaint!

December 21, 1943   Somewhere in England

Dear Fran,

Christmas is quite different in every respect. I may go Christmas caroling with our group. I do not know the details as yet. But I love the carols and I have heard none as yet. For one reason – our old ladies are so darn patriotic and conservative, they turn the "wireless" on twice a day for news and then they snap it off again. So that leaves out any possible chance of hearing carols by radio.

Last Sunday, three of us took it upon ourselves to take a four-mile – each way – walk to see one of our friends who was in one of the station hospitals as a patient. Quite a Sunday afternoon stroll – of eight miles at the very least. But we did enjoy it a lot. The country is so lovely here.

We had a mongrel dog that our boys have had as a mascot since the outfit organized – "Pudgy". Not a cute dog even, but the boys love it and she never leaves them – going on all their hikes and bivouacs, too. Anyway, they were determined to bring her over, so she was smuggled in their luggage! We all were so curious – doubting that it would work and yet we knew they would go to any extreme to bring her. And they did manage it! They nonchalantly carried her in a barracks bag as if she were luggage! The thing is, she was pregnant again (she had seven pups on maneuvers) and the boys figured that she should deliver on the 21st of December – today. And the latest news bulletin tonight was "five puppies and Mother and babies doing fine!" Pudgy picked out her 'master's' bed – Sgt. Morgan's - as a delivery table! And I went up to see her around noon when she had had only three – cute little things they are. But the fellows are all so pleased and interested!

Anything you buy Julia is okay by me. I trust your taste.

I know you had a nice Christmas and I hope Mother got my flowers and my cable for Christmas. Keep writing and give John my love when he comes home.

Love to all, Alice

December 25, 1943   Somewhere in England

Dear Julia,

The end of Christmas Day. And it did not seem any more like Christmas than Easter would! Please do forgive me if I let my hair down all the way, but I feel so blue and homesick and you are the only one I can really 'give forth' to, for I do try to keep my letters cheerful when I write home. And, as a rule, that is no trouble. But all I can do now, is think back and recall all of our former Christmases together, and then realize now what it is like here. Julia, I hope I never have to spend another Christmas away from the family. And yet, I fear I shall, for this is going to be a big job.

Now, would you be interested in how I spent Christmas Eve and Day? Yesterday, four of us, went to a close by town, for we were so blue, we had to do something. So, we went to a tea shop and had tea and toast. And then went to a show at the cinema, "The More the Merrier" (Joel McCrea and Jean Arthur) which was quite humorous and did cheer us up. Since there was no place open for supper, we found a fish and chips shop. I guess that is new to you. Let me explain. It is a very small shop with several tables and all they serve is fried fish, quite tasty, really and French fries (chips to you!) and tea or coffee. So, for us, that was our supper. Then we had to 'queue up' for our bus (line up to you.) When I got 'home', our ladies had hot chocolate and cakes for us in front of a fire, and do remember that milk and chocolate are scarce here, so that was quite a treat! And so, to bed at 11:00 p.m. Some Christmas eve!

Then this morning, we both slept until ten, at which time our lady awakened us to give us tea and jelly sandwiches. The high spot of our day was our most delicious and attractive Christmas dinner. Let me tell you a little about it. Hope I am not boring you. As a rule, we eat off bare, wooden tables, but today, we had white clothes and candles and what a difference that alone made. We also had lovely place cards, which I am sending you to keep for me. Our menu was fruit cocktail, turkey and dressing, giblet gravy, mashed potatoes, beans, corn, rice and bread and butter, coffee, pumpkin pie, candy and cigarettes – that was the end of our grand dinner. As I say, that was the real Christmas of our day. The next on our program was a party for thirty-five orphans and what darling children they are! Little and chubby and as cute as can be! And so affectionate! They were hanging all over our officers and boys. And they in turn, were so pleased and touched, for so many of them have youngsters at home and this is no easier for them to do, than for us. And the children were so thrilled to have the candy and cookies we had for them. It is so sad that they have no parents or love. That is the real sorrow of war. And so ended my day. I do realize that Christmas was no ideal day for you, but at least you are among your own people who have customs as you. What a difference that does make!

And now I sit in front of a fire and listen to two old maids talking – and that was Christmas for me. Oh, I did have one present to open from Ann. She mailed it on November 8 and I got it last night – a lovely Elgin compact. Quite different than I usually have. I am glad you got Mother the watch. Tell me a little more of it, please.

Well, thanks for listening to my tale of woe. And God bless you.

Love, Alice

"A very nostalgic day – our first Christmas overseas. Christmas had always been such a special holiday for us. Now I had to rely on my memories and I was so thankful that they were such good and such rich memories. On New Year's Eve, we were in a club and on the stroke of midnight, bagpipers came marching into the room. Such a mournful sound – but I loved it. This is a custom in Great Britain – and a very special one. I never hear bagpipes without remembering that night."

December 29, 1943   Somewhere in England

Dearest Mother and All,

I was so thrilled to get your v-mail saying you had finally learned that I was here in England. I know it must have been such a relief to you to know I was in the 'old country!' But I cannot quite make out why you have heard from me only once at the time of your letter of the 14th v-mail. For I wrote that letter after I was settled here and I have written you almost daily since we set foot on our boat to come over here. I guess our mail is the same as is yours. I receive mail that is dated early in November and in that same lot of mail, we will have mail written very recently. And, so it goes! But we welcome mail even if it were written a year ago!

I guess you have received my letter about my English Christmas. And I want to just forget that letter I wrote around Christmas, for I was feeling so blue and homesick and I should have had sense enough not to write it then. But I always feel better once I do write to either you or Julia when I am feeling that way!

I heard from Doris yesterday and she is expecting me on Sunday, so I shall write you all of the meeting after I come back from London.

I wrote to Aunt Maggie today and I am going to try to go over to Ireland to see her on my next three-day leave in February, if we are still here, and I hope we are. For I should hate to be so close and not go to see her. That would be quite something to be able to see her, wouldn't it? I asked her to write me and let me know where and how and such.

Yesterday, we got mail and how! I got seventeen, including several Christmas cards. How welcome mail is! I guess you look for my mail as anxiously and impatiently as I do from you. But do not write v-mail exclusively, please. Air mail is as quick in coming and seems so much more like real mail! But I am pleased with either. I also want to ask you one favor. Can you send me candy or gum and a little Kleenex . We can get only a little box a month here – now. You are allowed to send an eight-ounce package a week over, and we can get so little here. I know Frances would not mind sending this – it is her little contribution to the war effort. How about it, Fran? I'd do the same for you! And it is only once a week! Also, see if you can get candy over – we get so little sweet foods. Today we were fortunate and able to buy a pound box of candy – our own popular makes, as a Christmas gift to ourselves! Really, quite an occasion, too!

Last night our ladies had a tea for us and Christmas and had twelve there. She really is so sweet and goes to so much trouble, made lovely desserts and of all things – ice cream she made. We did not really expect to enjoy ourselves, but we did – quite. And it really is quite a job to get things here. Everything you can think of is rationed. Somethings you could not get for anything!

Well, Mother, how do you like your watch? I am sorry I could not help pick it out, but I am sure, from all I hear, it is lovely and I know you do love it. I'll have to wait until I return until I see it. Well, goodnight and keep up the good work. Write often and I will keep up from over here. Needless to tell you how I do miss all of you and hope and pray that this year shall see the finish of all this hatred and murder.

Love to all of you – Ernie, Ed, Fran and especially you Mother – Alice

February 15, 1944   Somewhere in England

Dear Mother and All,

Well, since I have not written home for four days, due to the fact I had my three-day leave and went to see Doris and Eileen. I'll try to make it up in this letter. To begin with, I had a wonderful time at Doris' home. It was next best thing, I feel, to going home. I couldn't have been treated any better by anyone outside of my own family. I just love Doris and Eileen. They are two lovely girls - refined and cultured and yet loads of fun and so likeable. They have that grand quality of making you feel at home and welcomed from the very beginning. Let me start from the beginning. It is easier and more coherent. The trip by train took only two and one-half hours and I made good connections, so I got to Newton Abbott by three thirty in the afternoon. Doris and Vivian, the little girl of four, were there to meet me and take me home. Doris certainly looked so smart - so unusual for what we see where we are, and is quite different. But she did look quite lovely and Vivian is adorable. Blonde with big blue eyes and rosy cheeks. And just as sweet as she is cute.

They live at Kingskerswell, which is about four miles out of Newton, on the way to Torquay and about halfway between the two. They rent a home here - a darling bungalow, furnished, as they have rented the family home furnished. But it is a lovely place, with three big bedrooms and a lovely living room. They have a lovely yard and gardens. I had a lovely, big room and a very comfortable and warm bed. And every morning, I had a cup of tea in bed! Eileen came home around five, from school, for she teaches children from three to seven years at Boscombe. She looks a little like Aunt Ruby and is a most likeable person. Also, the old father - he is a dear! Just a good and sweet old man of 75 and still on the old jog, too! They all seemed so glad to see me, sincerely so, too. I felt content and happy and right at home at once. Doris keeps a nice home and is a good cook too. She takes Harry's death so nicely, missing him so and knowing her future must be without him. Eileen and Ron make all their future plans to include both Doris and Vivian. They are really so close.

I took several lovely walks with them on the downs, which are so pretty, and I was quite fortunate in having lovely, sunny days while I was there. I also went twice into Newton and had tea in the nicest shop there – "Madge Mellars" by name. And then on Saturday, we took the afternoon and the four of us went to Torquay and later to Boscombe to the beach, and then to the hotel there on the cliff – Courtney Arms, I think it was called. It is a lovely place facing the ocean and from the window of the dining room, you can look out and see a great span of sea. It is a beautiful place. If ever I marry, I would love to spend my honeymoon right there. Quite serious, I am! I did enjoy the beach, too. It is so much prettier than our flat Jersey shores! I am sending cards home and please keep them together for me. Someday, I will enjoy looking over them.

As you can now gather for yourself, that I have had one grand time on my leave. I can say I have never been treated any nicer or better. I am so glad I did go down and I know, due to conditions, I would not have had as enjoyable a time if I had gone to Ireland. Eileen and Doris are lovely girls and I wish you would write them a note. They are going to write you, they told me.

They were quite sincere in asking me down whenever I could make it and even to bring a friend down with me. They are grand hostesses and if I have the time, I surely shall go again.

I gave Doris the pajamas and she was surely pleased. Also, Vivian, when I gave her the candy you sent me. It was their first box of candy in two years and Vivian took the cover off, looked at the candy and put the lid on again! She wouldn't eat any for quite a while. She was saving it! She is a darling. I took a few snaps. I hope they are good.

I wish you would do something for me if you can. Vivian has never had a doll with hair, so if you could find a small doll, cute, with hair, would you send it in the next box to me? I'd love to give her one. Something small of course, so it could be included in the regular size box. Also, some stockings – size 10, a few cotton and a few of nice rayon. We wear quite a few here. You may also send candy anytime you can get it. It is always a welcome box.

I had four letters today from Julia. She seems quite happy that she is to be transferred to Bethesda and so she should be. She is most fortunate.

I wish I could hear from home since Johnny was there. So far, not a word. The latest I have heard is the day before he is to arrive. I sure hope you have been writing anyway. Since I cannot be there, I at least would like to hear of all that was done while he was there. Details shall be appreciated!

Write soon and often, for I do love to hear all of what goes on.

Love to all always, Alice

March 3, 1944   Somewhere in England

Dearest Mother and All,

I fully intended to write you last night, but I was so tired after a full day of riding, I couldn't have possibly written anything. Several of us went to Taunton in a 2 ½ ton truck, and unless you have ridden in one, you would have no idea how hard the seats are or how cold the truck is, in spite of three wool blankets we had taken along. It was bitter cold and we were just about numb by the time we were halfway there – a distance of one hundred and fifty some miles round trip. So, we had the driver stop at the first tea room. It was ten in the morning and we went in – four of our enlisted men and three of us. The lady fixed us a most delicious cup of hot tea and cookies. It soon warmed us up and down to our toes! So, we asked the lady if we could use her bathroom. So, she took us upstairs and she went into one of the bedrooms and we dumbfounded when she came back with a china pot in each hand! And we couldn't very easily get out of it, for we really deemed it a case of necessity! The funny thing of it all was that the boys guessed it right away when we came downstairs laughing! "How were your accommodations?" was their question! But the tea did the trick and we remained quite warm until we arrived in Taunton. We went there to visit a hospital to see their surgical setup. All in all, we were riding from 8:30 to noon and 3:00 to 6:00 p.m. And we were tired!

Monday, we spend a week in the field. Brrr! I hope it is warmer.

I will ask for some candy and warm socks please. Cold feet are a problem. Take care of yourself.

Love always, Alice

March 11, 1944   Somewhere in England

Dearest Julia,

I know you must be disgusted with me for my seeming neglect of you this past week. But I do have a very good excuse. For you see we were out in the field all week. And we had exactly no time to write any letters. Am I excused? Thanks.

As I say, we were out in the field and set up our hospital complete. And now I do fully realize what a huge job and a big responsibility I have and I wonder if I am capable of it. But I know of no one else who can do any better. So, until they tell me, I shall keep on. I have been complimented by some of our officers on my "hard and efficient" work. And all of "my men" – sixteen in number, are apparently quite happy and satisfied with me and that means a lot to me. I have trouble with a few of the girls. I can expect that, I reckon. But we can simulate casualties through the O.R., scrubbed and all, and it is quite a job.

But we had a lot of fun in spite of hard work. We had a nice warm stove in our tents and our sleeping bags are so comfortable. In fact, we are warmer there than in our billets as a whole. And our food was good as a rule. I love this life, but it is so hard to dress cleanly. And our hands got so dirty!

Peggy sent a snap of Johnny. I guess you got one, too. It was good of the house, but rather dark of Johnny. I wish I would hear from him. I can't write ever as I have not his address.

Weren't the snaps of Ruth and Johnny cute? I love them. Ruth is such a dear and writes so nicely and often.

March 13, 1944   Somewhere in England

A break came here in my letter to you, for Captain L. called me and in order to make the Bristol bus, I had to hasten. So, I shall continue. I met Captain L. in Bristol and found him to be a very nice fellow. And a perfect gentleman in every respect. And after being taken for granted by our officers - for we are! It is indeed a treat to have someone treat you like a lady. By that, I mean of course, someone that seats you at a table and walks you across a street and all the other niceties that should be shown any lady. Anyway, we took the train to Stratford on Avon and arrived around 8:30 Saturday night. And we had made no reservations for sleeping that night! Crazy thing to do, but all of our plans had been so indefinite. So, we went to the Red Cross Club and the lady there scouted around the town and found us a lovely home to stay in. We were quite old-fashioned and took separate rooms! And we had our breakfast there. We stayed two nights. Fresh eggs both mornings! So, to you that would be no treat, but to us, it sure was! After eating powdered eggs for four months, you appreciate fresh ones!

We went to see all the places of interest – Shakespeare's home, Ann Hathaway's cottage, Mary Arden's home, Harvard House and Holy Trinity Church. They are so quaint and so old. The old beams and floors are pieces of art - much desired by antique collectors. I got, rather Captain L. got for me, some cards of the places. He wouldn't let me spend a cent. He bought even my return ticket - for he went on to

London and I returned to camp as he has the rest of his leave to spend in London. I'll send the cards to you and will you send them on to Mother, please.

I had not planned on staying over Monday, but it worked better as I would have missed the train to all the places of interest if I took the Sunday train back. And I was not signed out properly for Monday. So, I was rather uneasy about it. We are quite strict about signing out. But when I returned today to sign in, I was quite surprised to find congratulations awaiting me. For while I was away, my promotion had come through! I did not even know it had been started. So, in the future, please, I am your superior officer!

I have so many letters to write, I must stop now. Keep writing dear and I'll do likewise.

Love always, Al

March 14, 1944   Somewhere in England

Dear Julia,

You indeed must have had a premonition when you wrote your last letter to me – one which I received yesterday. In it, you made the remark that I would soon receive my first. And just a few hours before I received your letter, I was informed that effective March 1st, I was a First Lieutenant! Isn't that a coincidence! I mentioned it in the letter I wrote you yesterday, I know, but I just want to say a few more things, if you will forgive me for what may seem like self-praise. I merely request a few examples of what was told to me.

First off, our commanding officer, Colonial Johnson, stopped me yesterday at supper, took my hand and said, "I have been trying to find you to offer my heartfelt congratulations. I am very pleased at your promotion. If ever anyone deserved one, you did and I know of no one I would rather get it." I was so flabbergasted, for he is a G.I. if anyone ever was and I didn't realize he hew much about all I had done.

But it made me feel so good. And at this morning's breakfast, McLin, our chief nurse (she made a captain yesterday) gave me a pair of her sterling bars and Colonel Johnson pinned them on me. I am really fond of McLin. She is a decent person. If I may repeat another remark made, one of our officers told me I ought to have had it a year ago! And all of the nurses seem really pleased I have it. I know this sounds egotistical, but you will understand why I write this.

My leave has been changed until April 4th, 5th and 6th, so I guess I'll go down to see Doris then. I hope the doll Mother sent me for Vivian comes by then. Did you I tell you about that? I asked her to send one with hair as she never has had one. They don't make them here now, and Mother said she got a darling one in West Chester. I am anxious to see it.

Small world this is. Remember P.D. from Bragg? He is the fellow who wrote me for so long – the nice letters. Well, he is stationed about twenty miles from here. I wrote as soon as I knew and got a lovely, long letter from him. I may even try to see him, even if he is an enlisted man! He is a nice fellow.

Write soon again -

Love, Alice

April 3, 1944   Trip to Wales

Dear Julia,

I surely wish you could see us now! Three of us went to Cardiff, in Wales, today, to spend a day or so. We have a huge room in one of the old hotels, with two double beds, and believe it or not, ten mirrors of various sizes and shapes in the one room. So, every time you turn your head in a different direction, your image confronts you. We have pushed the two big beds together so we will not feel too lost and lonely. By the way, as a desk, I am using a bureau drawer removed from its moorings. Works quite well, too, if you ever want to try it!

Frankly, there is absolutely nothing to see here in Cardiff. It is quite an ugly place in the business area, and is quite a sea port town. We tried to go down to see the docks today, but had not gone very far in that direction, when two M.P.'s stopped us to tell us it was off-limits. I was getting sort of wary anyway, for there were all sorts and some were quite awful-looking. So, we turned back to a safer area. We then decided we would take a bus ride around to see the area around the city. We rode on the top deck and rode for around an hour and saw the residential area – very nice and clean. That called for supper on our return. So, we found a lovely place complete with music, a rare affair, and we had chicken for dinner! It was so good! And now, here we are, in bed and writing a letter. We are so tired, but glad we have seen Cardiff. Now that leaves only Ireland I have not been in of the British Isles. But they have been behaving so badly, I shall just ignore their presence.

This was just a note to tell you what I am doing. Keep writing.

Love always, Alice

P.S. Sure wish you were here to see all this with me. We'd have such a grand time together.

Alice, and her unit, spent a total of seven months in England preparing, practicing and waiting for the invasion into Normandy. Anticipation and tensions were high for soldiers and civilians alike.

THE INVASION

June 7, 1944   Somewhere in England

Dear Julia,

Well, the big day has finally come that we have all waited for so long. I can well imagine how all the folks back in the states are feeling now. And I only wish I could let Mother know now that all is alright here with me. For I fully realize it is going to be the natural thing for her to worry about me, thinking I am in the midst of it all. But I am not - yet. In fact, early in the morning of the invasion, I was awakened from my sleep by the sound of so many low flying planes. I got up to look and see what it was and what a beautiful sight I could see from my window! Hundreds of huge troop planes flying very low and with the red and green lights, flying in formation. Wave after wave of them flew over for hours and I sat there and watched them go off into the distance. But for some reason, I did not think they were the start of it all. They were though, for they carried the air-borne forces to Normandy. And in a few hours, I was again awakened to hear them return. Julia, awful as it was, meaning what it did, it was a beautiful sight and one to remember. So, you see, I saw the start of the Invasion and didn't even know it!

This morning, our entire outfit had a special prayer meeting and then after it was over, all who so desired, had the opportunity to partake of communion. I was so pleased they did it. I must say it did make you think a lot. I only hope this will be the step that will bring us home once again. It certainly has, in one way, relieved that awful tension and expectant waiting. Everyone is now so anxious to really pitch in and get it over with as rapidly as possible. We hate to be sitting back here, in the peace and quiet of England.

Enough of me and the war. Let us talk of more pleasant topics. For example, you and your friend, the Scotch doctor. I do so hope you got together and went hiking. He sounded so very nice to me. I can see now that you chose the proper service to join as far as male attention goes. We folks over here see only our own M.D. officers and a few line officers if you attend dances. And of course, our enlisted personnel. But they are so strict along that line. If you do date any, you have to be so sneaky about it and I hate that. But they need never think that will stop that sort of entertainment. It is too desirable at times to let any rule forbid. It goes on quite a bit, too, and more power to it! What say you?

In the future, any donations of food or candy will indeed be most welcome. If you can, send some candy or cookies of any kind. I'll do something, some day for you. Keep writing.

And love,   Alice

"I never stopped to rationalize that such a huge operation could ever be kept a secret. They were relying on the element of surprise. It was a solemn and tense time – for we were all aware that we would soon be very involved – and right in the middle of the action."

OMAHA BEACH, NORMANDY D-10

"Within the week, we left our peaceful village that had been our home for the past seven months. We drove down to Southampton on the southern coast to a huge staging area. After a few days of intense preparations, we boarded a large ship that would take us across the English Channel – to France! – and to the now famous Normandy Beach. We had boarded the ship at night, but we stayed in the harbor at Southampton until daylight. Naturally, we were all scared, nervous and anxious for we had absolutely no idea what lay ahead for us. No one knew – how could they?

The English Channel was full of ships of every description – war ships, troop ships, patrol boats – and the sky was filled with Allied planes. This was just ten days after the start of the invasion and we had no idea how the war was progressing, but we did know that we would be sorely needed.

As we approached France, after a very rough trip across the Channel, we could hear the bombing and the shelling nearby. In order to go ashore, we had to transfer to a smaller craft – L.C.T., standing for landing craft transport. That was quite an undertaking, as we all had to leave our larger ship by climbing down the side on rope ladders! We were now on Omaha Beach – and what a terrible sight it was. There were wrecked ships in the harbor and on the beach, and every description of vehicle and heavy equipment – in complete ruin all over the beach. The nearby hills were black from constant pounding from our big guns on the warships, and from the many tons of bombs that had dropped. And then we realized what tremendous loss of life – our men – must have taken place. The Germans had been fortifying the higher elevation for a long time. There was a huge line of concrete bunkers and they were in a perfect position to aim at our troops in comparative safety. It was a sight that could never be erased from your memory.

We had to remain on the beach for several hours until all our personnel were assembled. Not very far away, we could hear the terrible sounds of war – a sound that soon was to be a very big part of our life. We were still in a mild state of shock and unbelief at what we were seeing. Although we knew that we finally had arrived to do the work for which we had all volunteered and prepared for, it still seemed unreal. That did not last long, for we soon were on our way to an area several miles inland where we were to set up our hospital. We arrived in that area – it was full of bomb craters, fox holes and deep pits that the Germans had used for their gun emplacements – and so many trenches. They had indeed been well dug in.

We were exhausted and hungry, so we each picked a foxhole – at least this time we did not have to dig our own – and we got ready for the night. All we had with us were our personal belongings and a supply of our famous K-rations. We ate one of these and then got ready to spend a sleepless night in our foxhole.

But our Executive Officer arrived to inform us that the rest of our personnel and all our equipment – including our hospital – were still not unloaded. The channel was too rough. But we were all to go to a nearby area where an Evac Hospital that had arrived the previous day, was already set up and receiving heavy casualties – and needed help desperately.

So, we gladly climbed out of our foxholes and were taken to the hospital. We were happy to have something to do – and we certainly would feel safer here, for the planes were still bombing the area – snipers could be heard all around us. And we needed the experience before we set up our own hospital. It was providential, for there was so much we had to learn and there was no better way to do it. I went right on duty in their busy operation room, worked all night. The cases were horrible! These were the first true battle casualties we had seen- the first of many thousands we would see. I would never forget our initiation into war time nursing.

We remained with this hospital for a week as a storm was raging in the English Channel and the ships that were carrying our equipment and some of our personnel could not be unloaded any sooner. The experience we all received during that week was invaluable. Yet, how good it was to finally have our own hospital and personnel, and to begin to function as the 45th Evac Hospital."

An Evac Hospital operated and set up at the rear of the Front line and away from possible harm by the enemy ground troops. Although there was air activity overhead, there was relatively little risk to the 45th Evac Hospital. There was still "ack ack' fire fragments, firing of machine guns, mines and unexploded shells. The noise was intense and caused apprehension and fear, but there were no casualties among the personnel.

"As soon as we were completely set up, we were kept so busy, there was nothing but work and trying to sleep – in twelve-hour shifts. We would come on duty and there would be 150-300 casualties to take care of – and we could only run a maximum of twelve O.R. tables at one time, so we often worked longer than our twelve hours. There was so much to be done! As soon as patients left the O.R. for the post operative recovery wards, there were others to replace them. As I reflected on this, I did marvel how we did what we did – and again how thankful we were for that first week of experience we had. It was truly remarkable how smoothly everything seemed to run, for we had a fine staff and real team work.

Our first set-up was near a small French village – La Cambe – and I think it is important and interesting to describe our general hospital plan, for it was quite unique – so very different from the common concept of hospitals."

Convoy for the 45th Evacuation Hospital

The 45th Evacuation Hospital set up in field in Normandy

"We set up in a large open field. All our tents had large red crosses with white background to indicate from the air that it was a hospital and at either end of the hospital, there was another large banner on the ground with similar markings. This was necessary, for by the rules of the Geneva Convention, a hospital must never be bombed – and we never were."

The operating room "suite" was formed by placing four large ward tents together in such a way it formed a cross – all were connected in a way that everything was under one "roof". It was very complete – there were four separate O.R. rooms – each complete with three O.R. tables and a large central sterile instrument and supply table. In addition, we had another large tent for cleaning, sterilizing and storage of all the supplies. In this tent, we had a very faithful steam autoclave for sterilization, that was kept going around the clock. It never failed us. There was a scrub area with running water – quite a contraption – and a rigid sterile technique was strictly followed. It must again be emphasized that these were the days before any plastic, disposable supplies – everything had to be washed and sterilized after each use. How much simpler it would have been if we could have just thrown used supplies away and replaced them with sterile disposable items!

Adjacent to surgery was another large tent – or group of tents- for sick patients and triage. All incoming casualties were admitted here and evaluated for priority care. Each tent held about forty patients – and the overflow tents were usually also filled. It was so difficult to determine which patient received immediate care. (As we became more experienced, and when surgery was running smoothly, I had the responsibility of making that determination, for all medical officers assigned to surgery were needed in the O.R. It was too great a responsibility for any young nurse – there was just much to be done by too few people!) The enlisted medical corps men had been well trained in assisting the surgeon, so they were kept busy in this phase of the O.R. – the nurses were kept busy "circulating" and keeping everything running as efficiently as possible. It was remarkable, when you consider the complexity of most of the cases, and also the fact that we were usually very near the front lines.

Following surgery, patients were taken to either post-operative wards or shock wards for those who were in extreme shock. Most trauma cases were in very serious condition after surgery. How hard we all worked to save every life! But there were so many land mines and booby traps. Some of the patients never had a chance even if they had lived to reach the O.R. Never let it be said you can get used to anything – you cannot!

Most of the patients were traumatic surgical cases, but there were some medical cases to care for in a special area apart from surgery. These were dysentery, pneumonia, frost-bite, ulcers, etc., but it was interesting that there were very few stress-related cases, and very few drug-related cases. That was unheard of in our time."

It was difficult work and long hours giving care to their patients. Part of Alice's duties was to keep accurate and up-to-date records. Reviewing the records made the personnel more efficient and changes would be made in procedures to produce better outcomes for the patients. They were constantly readjusting the training they had had in the States to better accommodate where they were stationed and the number of casualties they handled. Personnel wanted to move patients through their hospital as promptly as possible so there would be no delay for incoming patients.

"In our first two weeks, we had about 1,200 trauma cases go through our O.R. And trauma cases are never simple surgeries. Each one seemed more complex and radical than the case before it. Evacuation hospitals cared for patients until they were ready to be transported back to the beach where they were taken by plane or ship to England to a Station or a General Hospital. (The use of helicopters for evacuation came at a much later time – during the Vietnam War.)

On a lighter note – our mascot Pudgy – had another litter of pups! She certainly does get around. These had to be English puppies.

We had assigned a small number of German prisoners of war who we used as litter-bearers and clean-up crew. They were well guarded – but they were happy to be with us – and we certainly needed them."

LA CAMBE, FRANCE

June 21, 1944   France

Dear Mother and All,

I sure wish I could write you a real letter, but due to censorship, I find it almost impossible to write a decent letter. But I do want to try to write as often as possible. I know you are worried now about me and I only wish I could reassure you and let you know I am alright. Please try not to worry, Mother, for I am quite well and happy in my work. And I am thankful for work now, for it is indeed a lifesaver.

We are in France, as you have already noticed from my heading above. It really is quite like any other country from all appearances, much like the part of England we left, in fact. I only wish my knowledge of the French language was a lot more. The other evening, two of us had a package of the noodle soup you sent me and it was the best thing I have tasted in a long time. Not that our meals are not good. They really are under these conditions. But we are eating field rations and if you know anything about these, you will understand. Hard-tack and canned foods exclusively! But I can easily see why foods are rationed at home. Please, never let anyone complain about any shortages there. If only they could see why they are rationed, they would never say a word. Our fellows over here are deserving of everything they get and so much more. They are doing such a grand job - the American soldiers, all of them, and so many are giving their lives in this invasion and others are physically handicapped for life. I never before fully realized the awfulness of war. You really do not, until you see it for yourself. The papers do not half tell you folks at home, what the score is. They paint quite an easy and optimistic outlook of all that goes on here.

I am afraid this does not seem like a very cheerful letter. I am sorry it isn't, but there isn't much cheerful about war, is there? Yet, I would not miss all this for anything. I'd do it all over again.

Ernie, I have never before been glad you were classified as 4-F. It may not be easy for you to take, but it is a blessing to Mother and all of us if you could only know it. People think the Japs are ruthless. Well, the Germans are equally so, if not more. Someday, I'll tell you all, what I can't say now.

Take care of yourselves – all of you and do not worry about me.

I would appreciate air mail stamps if you could enclose them in your letters. We can't get them here. Also, any donation of candy or cookies or soups. I hate to ask, but it does mean so much now.

Keep writing. It is not coming in to us yet, but one of these days, it is bound to come.

Love to all always,　　　　Alice

June 29, 1944　　　　　　　　　　　　　　　　France

Dear Julia,

Just a line, from behind the front line, while in the distance, I can hear the rumble of big artillery fire and see the tracer bullets they fire at these damn Jerries. No, I myself, did not realize we would be so close to it all. Do not tell Mom, of course, for I do not mention it to her! But we are between two airfields and the Jerries would love to have them. So, after dark, they come out and drop flares and our anti-aircraft batteries give them the works. And it is close! You can hear the shells whizzing over your tents and see the flashes of the big guns. Some nights, it is impossible to sleep. I was on night duty on the worst nights, so I was really quite fortunate. We are working very hard now, but it is so good to be able to take care of the fellows. They do appreciate it so. Someday, I'll tell you more of all they go through. It is a real hell!

It is getting dark and we can have no light after blackout hour, so I'll have to stop. I'll mail this just so you'll have heard from me. Keep writing, dear. I want so to hear from you – I haven't for a month now. I know you have written, but I got my first mail in a month today. It was wonderful!

Be good and keep writing and praying

Love always,   Alice

July 1, 1944   France

Dearest Mother and All,

Just another little note before I place my weary bones in my cozy bed roll. One of these days, when we have a lull period, I shall really take the time out and write you a really long letter. That is a promise.

It is good to be here to help these grand fellows. No one will ever know the feeling you have in doing so unless they go through it all. They appreciate it so and do feel better seeing an American girl. Then, too, they realize they are pretty safe when they see nurses, for they feel nurses would not be sent to any place where it wasn't safe. We have a wonderful group of fellows in our army. It makes you feel so badly to know all they are going through and wonder why? They are going through an awful ordeal and it is not all as bright and grand as the papers picture it. It is indeed, a veritable hell, no matter how you regard it. It is one thing to read about it and another to hear the actual story from them. Not one civilian can give up enough when you see all these fellows give up. I hope I never hear a civilian gripe or complain of what they sacrificed!

Sorry, I did not intend to write such as I did, but after seeing all those fellows come in surgery every day and hearing all they tell you, and seeing the results of war, there is plenty of reason for me writing it. I know you will understand.

74

It has been so good to hear from you. It means everything to me. And I do so want you to know I and all of our group enjoyed the noodle soup! It was wonderful! I still have quite a lot, but I'd love more when you can get it. I can get plenty of cheese. We eat a lot of it in our rations. I guess that is why it is rationed at home. But candy, cookies and perfume are always so welcome. Will that do for a request? I trust so.

I do not believe I told you I was sending a $25 War Bond home for Johnny for his birthday. I wrote him about it, but not you. I hope you have received it by now. Also, the extra $50 from my June salary, for I have no use for money over here in France. I want you to take $10 out of it for something for yourself. Please do this.

I was glad to hear my package came alright. I was afraid it might not. I am pleased you liked the ring, Fran. It was difficult to find a nice one, but I thought it was a dainty thing. But Mother, those spoons are for you! You keep them.

It is midnight and I'll have a busy day tomorrow so I must close – with all my love and may the same God who is keeping me from harm, watch over all of you and keep you for me.

Love to all always, Alice

"Our hospital was under the command of the First Army, so we moved forward as the First Army troops advanced. Sometimes, we would move 1-15 miles – other times it would be 50-100 miles. Everything depended on the progress the Allies made. We were always just behind the troops and always within earshot of the bombing, shelling, and anti-aircraft artillery. At night, we could see the huge searchlights sweeping across the dark skies, trying to locate enemy planes. Then our anti-aircraft artillery would zero in on the plane and we would watch the tracer shells – and hope they would hit their target – and that it would be an enemy plane. It was an awful sight to witness, but at the same time, it was really beautiful and breathtaking. There were also the flares dropped by the Germans in an effort to locate our army positions and the position of the ammunition dumps. We had seen direct hits on these ammunition depots and it is a spectacular sight – but an awful one.

We have heard shells whizzing over our tents frequently, and have seen the flashes of the big guns at night. No wonder it was difficult to sleep – no matter how weary we were. We often wore our helmets to bed, for we had shrapnel tear through our tents. That was a little too close.

What brave and fine young men our army had! They would go through our surgeries and so many would be disfigured and disabled for life. So many horrible injuries – yet they were so brave – and appreciated everything done for them."

July 13, 1944   France

Dearest Mother and All,

By now, I know you must have heard that I am in France, for I had a letter from Julia today and she had heard. And I wrote to both you and her on the same day. I have been most fortunate in receiving mail since I have been here, and it has meant so much to me to hear so often from the home front. I only wish I had had the time to write home more often in the past three weeks, but I know you will realize that it is only because I have not had the time or opportunity to write. We have been very busy since we arrived in Normandy, which was on D-10. It was quite a smooth trip over to France. The channel was quite quiet, thank goodness, and we landed in LCA's, just as you see in pictures. It really was quite an experience, and I must admit it gave us a rather odd feeling to realize we actually were on the beach head where so very few days before, such an intense battle had taken place. We saw such evidence of the conflict, but it was all de-mined and quite safe. We went to duty that night, and then and there, we had our first experience with actual battle casualties. And tired as we were from all the travel and tension, we were all very happy to at last be really doing the work we have wanted to do so long. It has been a hard job and very trying at times, but what a wonderful feeling to know we are really doing so much to help these fellows who are giving so much and doing such a grand job, even at such a great cost. What a wonderful group of soldiers we have!

To give you an idea of all we have done in surgery, we have had about 1,250 cases operated on in the past two weeks. And that is really, quite a number as you can easily understand. It has kept us on our toes and all in all, everything has been quite smooth, thank goodness.

Blackout time is here again. Time to go to bed as it is quite dark and all one can do is retire to your sleeping bag. All I want to add now is, to ask you please not to worry about me as I am really alright and quite safe. I will write you as often as I can and I am looking forward to all your letters, so keep writing.

Take care of yourselves, all of you, and may God be with each of you, no matter what the outcome is.

Give everyone my love and explain why I do not write. Give Ruthie my love and I'll write as soon as I can.

Love always, Alice

"As we moved through France, we were frequently able to take time to meet some of the local farm families as our hospital was usually near a village. And they loved "us Yanks!" for we were there to free their country from the enemy. There was never any question about the United States succeeding in doing that, so we were always welcomed. As the situation permitted, we left camp to find a farm where we had learned to barter for fresh eggs and laundry service. Fresh eggs were such a treat – all we had were dehydrated eggs and they were a poor substitute. We had no decent or satisfactory way to launder our fatigues – except by hand in a helmet filled with cold water. The farm people were so happy to accept payment in soap, coffee, cigarettes and sugar. These were things that were non-existent now in their lives. We were always fortunate in locating these services, and although we often stayed a short time in one place, we were always able to pick up our uniforms before we left. There were some very close calls – but we never had to leave without them. We always found the farmers fundamentally good people who loved their country.

In July, we moved frequently – long distances each time. This was a sure indication that the front was advancing rapidly – and this was encouraging news. As we were close to our troops, that also meant we were near the front line.

In late July, we were located near St. Lo, when a very large number of Allied bombers started to pass directly over us. We were just preparing to move forward to a new location, so our hospital was already down and on the truck. We later learned that there were about 3,000 planes that were going over to the German lines. It was an unbelievable sight as we watched them pass directly over us. Then we could hear them "laying their eggs" (the army terminology, not mine- for I hate the phrase!) and we could actually feel the earth tremble from the continuous bombing. Talk of "overkill" – this was a perfect example. All we could think was "Thank God they are our planes!" To say we were not scared would not be true. We were all scared so many times. (no wonder I hate all the noise and lights of all 4th of July celebrations. The first time I spent that holiday in the States after I was discharged, I admit I was terrified – as all the memories of the war flooded back so vividly.)

We later learned that St. Lo – now a pile of rubble – had been fiercely defended by the Germans for two months. In eight days, our army broke through their lines. St. Lo went down in history as a great battlefield, but all that was left of the greatness was a cathedral – not completely leveled – standing in its own rubble. This was what we saw several days later when we passed through – and not one sign of life.

This broke the bottleneck that had existed for two months, and when our troops broke through, they were able to sweep all the way across France in pursuit of the German Army. A victory — but what a terrible loss of life — German and Allied."

AIREL, FRANCE

July 29, 1944   France

Dearest Julia,

I just received your letter of July 13 - pretty good service over, isn't it? Our mail service really is good. I do not know what we would do if it were any other way.

I am going to ask you not to let Mother see this letter, please. For if she were to read it, I know she would worry, but I want to talk with someone and you are the logical one. I would love to tell you all in detail, but I guess censorship would forbid that. The thing I want kept from Mother is the fact that we are so close to the front. Try to convince her we are quite a way behind, will you? It may make her feel better. Even we are surprised that we are so close. I can't say how close, for they move around so, but did you read in the papers about the huge air armada of about three thousand planes that went over to German lines about three days ago? Well, they all went directly over our field. It was indeed a wonderful sight to see. I had read before of a thousand planes going over, but three thousand and to actually see it! We could hear them "laying their eggs" and feel the concussion caused by them. All I can say is - Thank God they were our planes! But at night, Jerry comes over and always, it seems, picks out our field to fly over. And then all our anti-aircraft guns open fire on him. Julia, you're never been scared until you have been through this. I am far from a cow-ard, you know that, but I sure am scared when the flak starts flying around and whizzing by you in the dark! And then you can see Jerry deposit his bombs in the distance - a huge area of red glow in the sky. Beautiful really, but how horrible! The whole sky lights up and then you know what the cause is. And on the way over, they will drop flares to see to take pictures for future reference. It is exactly like the huge

Fourth of July fireworks, only you realize what it all means, it loses its attraction. But I will say, there is not one of us who is not scared and who doesn't "hit the dirt" when they start!

Of course, you realize that this is only for you. Please do not let any of the others read it. They would only worry. I don't want you to worry, but I had to write you anyway! And I still wouldn't have missed it or wouldn't trade it for the world! Quite a queer person I guess I am!

Must hurry and go on duty – getting late, but do write. I am still wondering what is going on as far as your romance is concerned. I am really very interested in hearing and I only want you to be happy.

Love Always, Al

P.S. How about sending me some candy.

August 7, 1944   France

Dear Mother and All,

Once again, we are settled for a few days of rest, having just arrived at a new area about twenty miles from our last area. It was a long and hot ride and it was wonderful to have our tents up and water for a "helmet bath". I now feel quite refreshed again and ready for a few letters. I do not know if you folks realize what our outfit does – moving around so much. It all depends on how fast our troops move forward. The more progress they make, the more forward moves we have to make in order to take care of our wounded. And lately, our troops have made such rapid progress, we have had to keep on the move. So, we are getting a chance to see the country. And we see it very spoiled after it has been taken by the Allies – a city which very recently fell to the Allies – a city you have read a lot about, no doubt, in the papers. I never thought I would see a city so utterly and completely demolished. There was not one sign of life remaining in the area, and hardly one brick on the other. It was absolutely awful to see. And in all the ruin, you could see how strongly fortified and "dug in" the Germans were. It was quite a victory for our side and paved the way to Paris. But it surely was a ruined and deserted city. It was heartbreaking to see all the homes on the way so utterly and absolutely destroyed – some lovely homes, too. Folks at home see pictures of the war in the papers and read of it, but little do they, or can they, realize how terrible war really is. No one could until they see it for themselves. A truer statement was never made than "war is hell". I will be so glad when it is all over, and that should be soon, and I can go home and dress like a lady again. I wouldn't want to leave until it is over, but it will be wonderful to wear a feminine outfit again instead of fatigues, leggings and helmets! You folks at home can start any time at all to get me some pretty, feminine articles of clothing at my expense, instead of trying to send me any presents this Christmas.

I hope you are completely well again and do take care of yourself and write when you can.

Love Always to All,   Alice

SAINT-SEVER, FRANCE

August 16, 1944   France

Dearest Julia,

I only wish I could tell you how much it means to me to see a letter from you amid all the pile of mail for nurses. It puts the right finish to any day, no matter how hard or trying a day we put in, and between thee and me, many a day that are so. For Julia, it is so hard to see these fellows come in all banged up and hopeless cripples for life – fellows who will never walk again, or speak again, or to see a one good-looking fellow lying on a table with his face shot away and so many awful things you would never even think could be possible. To see that day after day, and then stay awake practically all night due to the planes and guns so close by, is almost as much as you can take. So please, dear, if my letters frequently sound unlike me, it is for that reason and no other. I get a certain sense of relief after writing to you, for I feel that no matter what I write you, you will understand why. I never write so to Mother, for I do not want to trouble her. I figure she worries enough as it is. Enough of me – I am fine, and we are quite slow right now.

Julia, if you are really in love with this fellow, for your own sake, do not consider it so impossible a situation! Better to love a fellow younger, than marry an older person you would not feel so about. Goodness, Julia, love is not so common a thing as all that. And fine, decent fellows are not common finds either. Take your happiness while you can. I know I would. I learned a lot the hard way.

Yesterday, a lot of us bought paratrooper boots. You know what I mean? – from a mobile PX and you should see us! If ever I can wear heels again, it will be a wonder! But I am so tired of leggings and these do look nicer. We sure are far from female in our appearance. I am glad no one that knows us can see us! Fatigue suits and leggings! How awful is our uniform! But how practical too. There is no glamour in an evac hospital! In spite of it all, we manage to remain quite happy and sane!

Thank you for the box of cologne and lipstick – and I'll always welcome perfume when you can send it.

Be good dear, and write and tell your sailor I am all in his favor and wish him luck! I only envy you!

May God keep you and bless you always, Julia dear.

Love Always,   Alice

As the First Army advanced on the Front, the 45th Evacuation Hospital moved closely behind them. They were the first line of medical aid behind the front line. They could always hear the fighting going on. It was so horrible, but Alice felt so good knowing she was doing good. War is hell and they saw it first-hand. When asked decades later, "Did you ever imagine in nursing school that your medical career would take you to something as horrible as that?", Alice's answer was, "You can't imagine anything being that horrible!" Here, she was 24 years old, in charge of not one, but 8-12 operating rooms at one time! She did 12-hour shifts of setting up, taking care of patients, then going to bed. Sometimes days shift, sometimes night shift. Alice thrived on the work and wrote letters home to family almost every day – quite often writing by candlelight. She was very limited in what she wrote. She couldn't mention anything about her location or war activity. She would write about her day and what she saw on leave. She thought once the war was over, she could tell them everything when they were together again. She wouldn't allow herself to cry, as she felt once she started, that she would not be able to function.

The medics at the front gave fluids and applied massive bandages on the wounded and got them transported to the evac hospitals as quickly as possible. The evac hospitals were likened to emergency rooms in our hospitals. In addition to administering, readying equipment and personnel, and O.R. service, Alice was constantly packing, unpacking and setting up the operating rooms. The enlisted men were trained to assist in the O.R. Alice would do triage, deciding which patients received care first. Alice said she had much more responsibility than she ever should have had. You had to be efficient in what you did. Patients generally stayed with the evac hospital 4-5 days. They wanted to evacuate them back to hospitals in England, because they were constantly moving. They never took a patient to their next location. Alice would not allow herself to feel despair, because she was not facing what these wounded soldiers would face if they survived.

When the 45th evac moved to Senoches, they lost its 60 German P.O.W.'s that had previously been assisting in putting up the hospital tents and being litter bearers. When the hospital used prisoners for labor, they were guarded by someone belonging to the unit's personnel. The loss of these prisoners, put a much greater burden on the enlisted men.

SENOCHES, FRANCE

September 3, 1944 Labor Day   France

Dear Mother and All,

What a lovely fall day this is! A little too windy for comfort, when one has to live in a tent, for unless everything is securely anchored, it will soon be winging its way to other parts of the field. In fact, several times during these past few days, I was sure our whole tent would itself take off! But it is such a grand change after rainy weather and the sun is so lovely and warm during the day. And at night, we are now having a full moon. You really couldn't ask for more perfect weather.

I received two packages from you yesterday – one with tea, soup, and crackers and the other with prunes, raisins and sardines. I can assure you we shall indeed enjoy it all. I was down to my last package of soup as I had taken it on duty at night in surgery and made a pitcher of it for the boys and us. It surely makes a hit - especially around 11:00 p.m. on a cold night! I have an unusually good bunch of fellows to work with - they appreciate little things like that. We receive a monthly liquor ration of a quart of whiskey and a pint of gin. Only officers, of course. The men receive nothing for some reason. So, I am giving mine to the fellows. They have been drinking French liquor and cognac, so at least this is a good brand of liquor. Somehow, if they are going to send liquor rations, it only seems fair to me some sort of an allowance ought to be made for the men – in place of nurses and Red Cross workers anyway. It makes the fellows rather bitter.

Yesterday, a group of us had the treat of going to see a French chateau fairly close by. It was beautiful. Completely furnished and just recently vacated. The Germans had lived there as a headquarters for quite a time and only vacated it two weeks ago when they were forced to retreat. So, a group of our army officers have lived there in luxury for almost two weeks. The place itself looks quite modern in spite of the fact it was originally built in the 1700's and remodeled inside in 1938. The furnishings are exquisite! All of the lovely furniture and tapestries and rugs and draperies are exactly as when the family lived there. Huge and beautiful tapestries covering one entire wall of a very large room. It must have been worth a fortune. And the master bedroom – a dream in pale blue satin – bed, chaise lounge, drapes and chairs. A typical and utterly feminine room and how out of place men's big boots looked under that bed! And army attire hanging in one of the many closets that literally lined the room. Closets in which, by all rights, feminine creations from gay Paree should be hanging! And the adjoining dressing room in gold and white – full of mirrors lining the room. And adjoining that – a blue tile bath room. What a treat to sit on a real "johnnie" that you could flush and get up without the lid automatically falling down, hitting you as you arise! And to look at a tile wall instead of a canvas tent wall! And also, how out of place a pair of leggings looked soaking in one of the lovely white wash basins! That was the master bedroom, occupied now by a colonel in our army. There were many other bedrooms, all with connecting baths – all simply beautiful – one in pink, one in yellow and odd as it may seem, one done beautifully in red tile with red candlewick drapes. And another bedroom done in orange. But it was lovely.

Then the grounds were lovely and kept by a caretaker who still lives on the grounds in a darling little home that looked more like a chateau than the main house. A lovely lake at one corner of the grounds and a tennis court behind it and the entire home surrounded by a small moat. Lovely flowers and bushes and in all, it gave the appearance of a well-kept modern estate – a far cry from war and destruction that you passed continuously in order to reach the chateau. Village after village in ruins and yet not a sign of war in any of the areas near the chateau. It was a grand trip and I was very glad of the chance to go. I would not have missed it for anything. By the way, the owner of the place – one of five homes, is the owner of glass and munitions plants. Quite similar to DuPont in our country. I do not recall his name, but he surely must have the shekels!

And another grand treat yesterday was to see lights – the first since we left the state, and that is really a long time! From Cherbourg to Paris, all vehicles may have lights on instead of driving under blackout conditions. It is wonderful to see bright lights coming over the crest of the hill. And homes with lighted windows. How I hate blackout! When I get home, I am going to turn on every light in the house and leave all the venetian blinds open!

You asked me about size – I'm afraid I have not changed one way or the other – size 36 – so if you see any pretty slips or such, put them aside for me. Because I'll want some pretty things!

It is so windy, I have twice chased this letter, so I guess I have written enough. I sure hope all is well at home. I try to write as often as possible, but with blackout so early, it is hard to at night, so do not worry if I do not seem to write as often as you'd like.

Take care of yourself – all of you and God bless and keep you safe for me.

Love Always,   Alice

PARIS, FRANCE

"As we sped across France, we went through Paris. In fact, we stopped during the night and actually camped overnight in Paris – yes, right in one of the little parks just off the street! Of course, our Executive Officer knew where we were, but we did not – we just climbed into our sleeping bags and slept. That was our initiation to Paris – city of Lights and Love.

A short time later, after we had set up our hospital on the other side of Paris, we were on a rest period and were given a three-day pass to go to Paris. Even during the war, it was a very beautiful city – and no longer occupied by the Germans. The war had not really physically touched Paris, for it was a specific order of the German commander not to bomb the city – but to keep it unscathed. He had a great appreciation for the beauty and great treasures of this old historic city. How much the French people owed to that great officer!

While we were in Paris, there was a great parade to celebrate the liberation of the city. This was a wonderful time for the French people and they were jubilant. The famous Champs Elysees was lined with the happy people of Paris, and there were many allied army personnel in the crowd. Both General Eisenhower and President De Gaulle headed the parade – down through the Arc de Triomphe – very appropriate. It was such a thrill to be able to be a part of this great and happy celebration. How proud we were – for this was our General!

Before we had left to come to Paris, we had been told by our officers who had recently been in the city, that we could barter for anything we wanted – using cigarettes in the place of money. As neither Vicky or I smoked, we had gathered our rations of cigarettes – we each had about six cartons – and took them with us to Paris. We had no idea why we had saved our cigarettes – perhaps this was why.

In Paris, we headed for Guerlain's House of Perfumes – the most exclusive one in Paris. But when we had selected our perfumes, we just could not bring ourselves to barter in such an elegant place. So, we paid for our purchases in francs, took our perfumes – and cigarettes – and left.

A G.I. who had been observing us, and realizing that we had not been able to go through with bartering – something he could never understand – offered to help us get rid of the cigarettes. He told us to stay where we were and wait for him. In no time, there was a large crowd of well-dressed people around him. In less than ten minutes, he returned with a huge wad of bills (francs) – and no cigarettes. We told him to keep the money, that he had earned it – and we were embarrassed by it all. He would not do this and asked us if there was anything we wanted, but found hard to get. We told him 'film' – so off again he goes and shortly returns with a large supply of film. We did insist he keep the remaining money – still a large amount. That G.I. knew his way around – a young entrepreneur!

Then, like the Pied Piper, men and women began to follow us, thinking we had some special source of Yankee cigarettes. At least we had our perfume to send home as gifts as soon as possible – and we had gotten rid of those cigarettes!"

Alice with her unit in front of the Arch De Triumph in Paris. Alice is 7th from the left in the back row – the very short one!

On The Champs – Elysees – just before the Big Parade – with Eisenhower and De Galle!

Waiting for the parade to start on the Champs Elysees

September 16, 1944   Belgium

Dearest Julia,

It has been so long since I have received any mail. I have had
to resort to reading your old letters. It has been over three weeks since
we have received any real mail and we certainly do miss it. Mail is our
mainstay over here, as I have written to you so many times you must
tire hearing it. But every day we are so hopeful, that when we do get
our mail, we shall have so much of it. You sort of lose your incentive
for writing when it seems so one-sided, so that would account for the
fact I have not written you for some time. I really am ashamed, for in
the past ten days, I have written exactly one letter – to Mother – but I
sort of make up for not writing by making a sixteen-page letter, all
about my trip to Paris, and a few other events, and she will send it on
to you, for I cannot repeat it all again in a letter where I had known
you would read her letter anyway. But I loved Paris. No other city I
have ever been in can start to compare with it. And so, you can imagine what a lovely place it must be in time of peace. But odd as it may
seem, war certainly seems far removed from Paris. Very little damage
has been done to the city itself and it is certainly well on its way to be
"back on its feet" again.

I had no way of getting you a present for your birthday any
sooner, but while I was in Paris, I got you some real French Parisian
perfume. I want you to realize that it is good, for in Paris, Guerlain's
is one of the best perfume houses and this particular one has not as yet
been sent to the States, so it is strictly French. I do hope you like it. I
have sent it on to Mother in a box of other perfumes I got for Mother,
Fran, Ruthie, Rose and Goldie – just small ones for them, but really

nice ones. Mother will send it on to you. I do hope it reaches you in good condition.

September 17, 1944   Belgium

A very rainy afternoon, but a wonderful day to write and as things are not too busy in surgery, I can give the girls two hours off and take the same myself. Oh, I forgot to head this letter properly, after 17 September. I ought to have put – "somewhere in Belgium". Isn't it remarkable how I manage to get around! We had a beautiful trip across Belgium. I guess we soon will be in Germany and then Berlin. And then I only hope – home. If only we are not sent to China or Japan! I hardly think we will, but one never knows in the Army. After having no mail for so long, I got five from you today and some from home and Ruth and Reilly. And I also got a box from you with the Cara Nomi cream, powder and the candy covered nuts. Thanks, dear. It was so sweet of you.

Belgium is a very lovely country – so beautifully scenic and clean. The homes are spotless – such a contrast to the French and also much more modern. Homes in some places are as modern as our most modern ones at home. It is a very prosperous looking country, too. Scotland, England, France, Belgium – then Germany, I guess. Wonder where else before I return to the most lovely of all countries, the U.S.A. Julia, it will be wonderful! You will never know, I hope.

Keep writing and be happy and you know how to do that! Love always and may God bless you,   Al

EUPEN, BELGIUM

September 28, 1944   Belgium

Dearest Mother and All,

Night duty again and a very quiet one at that. It is now 4:30 and just the time of night when I start to get sleepy unless we are very busy. And we are not. Just enough to keep us going and awake. I am glad for one thing only when we are not busy and that is the fact it means our casualties are light. We set up yesterday for the first time in a building! And what a wonderful change that is after the mud and cold of a tent! It will be that way from here on, too. No more tents for the winter - too hard on personnel and patients. The building we are now in, was formerly a Nazi Youth, or rather Hitler Youth school. It is very modern and, I have never seen any school more fully and beauti- fully equipped – every article of the very best and complete. The school itself is large and airy and ideal for a hospital. When we first arrived, it was full of school desks and books, and also German articles as they had used it for quarters for a month. So, a detail of German prisoners cleaned it out and while they were doing it, we made a tour of inspection of the place. Beautiful tile floors and clean painted walls – large windows with green fiber shades, the roll-up kind, you know. The furniture is all new and so very good. And such very beautiful oil paintings on all the walls. In short, we have a lovely place – just like a civilian hospital, especially surgery. It is so nice to have a tile floor and big windows and even the ideal green walls and cabinets in place of boxes. The only objection to it all is the fact it takes a lot more work to set up for only an average of ten days. And also, getting used to the hard floors, for our legs and feet get so tired now. Quite a change after spongy ground.

I wish you would try to get to see a copy of September's Vogue magazine, for in it is an article by a correspondent who was visiting us for an article on evacuation hospitals and although our name is not mentioned in it, it is our hospital she writes about. I have not read it yet, but they say it is quite good.

Well, I hope all is well at home and I am so glad to hear you are taking care of yourself and not over-working too much. I only hope it will soon be over and we'll be together again. That is all any of us here want and soon.

Love to All,   Alice

"This would be the longest time we had been in one place – about three months. And it was a great set-up, for it was in a large, modern Nazi Youth Training School – near the German border. In addition, there was very adequate room to house all the nursing personnel. Such luxury! We soon found that hard floors were the least of our worries. We were so busy with casualties here – the Germans were really now pushing hard and we were expecting a big offensive soon.

I could not believe my eyes when one day – in the afternoon – as I was lying in bed trying to sleep, as I was on night duty – I looked out my window and saw a German plane flying so low, I could easily see the German cross on the fuselage! It must have been a surveillance plane, for shortly after this, the activity increased.

Several nights later, we had indefinite warnings from local residents, who were requesting to use the large air raid shelter in the basement of the school. That night, we realized we were in for some activity. We watched as in the distance, the German planes began to drop flares. As I stood on the table in front of one of the windows in the hallway of the second level, I watched it all. I did not know the flares were from German planes – and I was fascinated by the beautiful display. And I was stupid. As they came closer, we were all ordered to the bomb shelter. There was no hesitation now, for we now realized we were under attack!

There were a few patients who could not be moved, so minimal staff remained with them. We would have to wait until morning to learn how close it was.

Much too close! At daylight, we learned that all the glass in the windows was shattered and there were large pieces of shrapnel through many of the wall and ceilings, and all the plaster had fallen from the walls. It was a mess and we were fortunate as there were no casualties. But when we looked outside, we could not believe the sight we saw – for our hospital was circled by big bomb craters – really huge ones. The hospital itself had not taken any direct hits, but as far as we could see, there were huge craters everywhere. The few patients were frightened, but not hurt. In the field, they could always look for cover – but here, they could not even get out of bed.

This was our closest call during the war – and it was proof that the enemy did honor the large red crosses we always displayed on our hospital. We were not their target, but two large ammunition depots about three miles away."

School that housed the 45th Evac

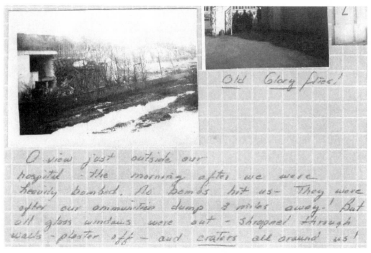

Old Glory flies!

A view just outside our hospital - the morning after we were heavily bombed. No bombs hit us- They were after our ammunition dump 2 miles away! But all glass windows were out - Shrapnel through walls - plaster off - and craters all around us!

Bombed out area outside of school

The 45th Evac did come under enemy fire and ground attack with the German counter-attack. They had to release the P.O.W.'s and the personnel were limited to the hospital area. Eupen experienced enemy artillery fire. One shell exploded a few feet from one of the buildings. The hospital sustained no damage however. A fuel depot nearby blew up. The force blew out all the windows and the nurses' rooms had evidence of machine-gun fire and there was debris everywhere.

October 10, 1944   Belgium

Dear Mother and All,

Another quiet night almost over. It is good mainly for the reason that it means our casualties are light and is always good news. The cases we have received are, more or less, minor ones on the whole. I only wish that could continue, for our men have gone through enough already. We are now wondering if only a real spring offensive will bring this mess to a close. Looks like we shall "dig in" here for the winter. We are so thankful we are in warm and dry buildings for the cold days. It is going to mean a lot to all of us. And we are more than fortunate to have gotten a new and modern building. I have no idea how long we shall remain here.

I guess all my letters seem full of only myself and my doings. After I mail them, I realize this - that I scarcely mention you folks at home - to ask about you and what you do or think. Please do not feel it is that I am not interested, for I truly am. I think about all of you so much, believe me. But when I start writing about it, it just makes me homesick. I know you will understand how I feel. Especially with winter coming on and that means another Thanksgiving and Christmas away from all of you. And, believe me, they are not easy to take under such circumstances!

But I must not go on in this frame of mind. For I am happy that I can be doing what I am for the fellows. One of the litter bearers from our outfit attached to us just told me the fellows had taken a vote tonight and selected me the "sweetest and best nurse" here. I consider that a great compliment, for they surely do talk the nurses over - pros and cons. Little things like that are so encouraging, too. We need them to help us along.

Today, I received my first package from you in months. It had the two magazines and the glasses, powder and paper. Thanks for everything. It was wonderful.

I have quite a few cards of Paris and Versailles that I am going to send over to you. They are really lovely. Also, a few hankies I got for souvenirs - nothing much, because we couldn't buy them without points (so we thought while we were there).

Well, good night all of you and I only hope and pray you are all well and stay that way. Write when you can and make that often! Give everyone my love and I'll try to write them soon if time permits.

Love to all of you always, Alice

Give Ruthie my love and tell her these letters are written to include her always

November 5, 1944   Belgium

Dear Mother and All,

Yesterday, I heard from both you and Fran and I was certainly glad to hear, for it has been well over a week since I had last heard from you. And I have not heard from Julia for even a longer time. Mail has been very irregular lately and although we can expect it to be that way, it is so disappointing to receive no mail. And the same with packages you sent. I have gotten none for about six weeks. So, you can see, the mail situation can leave much to be desired, but after all, mail of a necessity must take a place in the background.

In your letter yesterday, you said you had gotten the Parisian perfume. I am so glad, for I was beginning to think that it may not have gotten to you at all. It may be different from what you are used to and prefer, but I have found that just a few drops of it, it is really nice. It is quite concentrated and takes very little.

You made a very accurate supposition, in regards to our location. I often wonder how much you hear of what really goes on over here. It is not to be expected that you hear even half of it, of course. I was talking to a patient the other day. He had attended West Chester Teachers College and lived in west Philadelphia. He only came over two months ago. He said that the people at home do not begin to realize that there is a war going on! Their only indication of one is the scarcity and rationing of a few articles. I would hate to think this was so, but I somehow feel it is. If only they could see a little of what I see, and I see comparatively little, they would know. Young men going out to die fighting for what – folks at home to have a good time! And if they do not die out there, they may be completely crippled or maimed. Pardon me if I seem to rave, but things like that just start me off, especially when after hearing that, they brought in two young fellows – traumatic amputation of both legs for each of them. Unfortunately, they didn't live very long, but if only those people back there, safe and secure, warm and comfortable, could realize all this, I guess they just do not want their happy life disturbed! Please do not think I ever mean you folks. You have a great knowledge of what I mean, I know. Forgive this tirade, but war is too close and real for us.

Keep writing and do keep yourself well. I am fine, so do not worry about me.

I must report on duty now, so goodbye for now.

Love always to all,   Alice

November 26, 1944   Belgium

Dear Mother and All,

Only now do I realize how long it has been since I last wrote a letter and I feel badly about it. But I have been so tired and so busy, I just could not bring myself around to writing. And now I am on night duty again, so I usually find I have more time on nights to write. Writing during the day, of course, for our nights are busier than daytime is. But I have always found I have more time for such things when I am on night duty. Then too, I have had only one letter from home – one from Fran two days ago – in almost a month. I have not even heard from Julia. I was quite worried, for I was afraid something was wrong at home. Now I try to feel it must be due to all the Christmas mail rush. I did send a cable to you about two weeks ago, but it seems they are quite slow in arriving. But do not worry about me, for I am fine - just quite weary of war. I never realized it could get you down so completely, but twelve full hours of seeing our young men come in so frightfully wounded, and it has been a steady diet of just that for almost six months now, is really hard to take. I often wonder how I can go back to civilian nursing and cater to neurotics after seeing how wonderful our boys can take such terrific suffering. I guess that is something that time alone will have to work out.

Well, another Thanksgiving Day has come and gone and may it be the last away from home. We had a very delicious dinner though, turkey and all the trimmings - and our cooks did a wonderful job. But Thanksgiving is a day to spend at home and always shall be!

It appears that the Germans are making one final futile, but terrific last stand in an effort to save their wonderful fatherland! Oh, they are a ruthless race! They stop at nothing!

But I did not want to write this sort of a letter to you. I start out with such good intentions of not mentioning war and its horrors, but I guess I am too much a part of it to ignore it. Forgive me please!

From the description of the new wallpaper, it must be lovely! How I long to be with all of you again - safe and content in a pretty home! How much all of the little things that you take so for granted, would mean to me now!

I do hope all is well with all of you. Please take care of yourself, Mother, and Ernie, for you are the two I am most concerned about, from past experiences.

Please write soon and often, for you have no idea how I have missed hearing from you these weeks!

Love to all of you always and God bless you,   Alice

December 27, 1944   Belgium

Dearest Julia,

I have been trying to write you for five days now, but something always manages to interfere. Here is hoping I can both start and finish this letter at the one sitting. There is so much I want to say and tell you. What I would give for a good talk with you!

Well, Christmas has come and gone, and hardly does it seem that it was ever Christmas to me. We had a lovely tree and a delicious turkey dinner, but it certainly takes a great deal more than that to make Christmas, doesn't it? I worked all Christmas morning and had the afternoon off as we were too busy. Two poor fellows had their leg - each one – amputated and somehow that started my day off wrong. No matter how many times I see an amputation, I shall never be used to it. It always hits me hard, especially when these young kids take it so well. Where they get all their spunk and courage, I shall never understand. They deserve all the credit and praise coming.

Our whole week before Christmas was a hectic one. One which somehow brought the war so much closer to us than the other six months had. We learned what a bombing really was by experience, what strafing was like and what it was like to spend the nights in air-raid shelters. It is so plain that the Germans are coming out in the open now as a final, desperate stand. But you have no doubt read all about it in the papers there. It hasn't been a very pleasant feeling – not knowing where they would draw the line, for they are so ruthless. As a result, we are all sort of on edge and not a very merry group. If only it all were over and we could once again relax and be in a happy and peaceful world with our own kind of folks! Julia, I have been so home-sick and blue lately and just long for the day peace is declared and all that it means. To be able to sit down in front of an open fire with all your family there and know that only my own choice will take me away from it all. To be with people who talk and think and like the same things you do. To be able to go to bed at night and to know your peace will not be disturbed by enemy planes flying over and artillery fire shaking all sleep out of you. In short, Julia, I want to see this war over and soon! I hate everything about it now!

But enough of that, I ought never to write you such thoughts, but I feel better after writing it.

I want to thank you for the watch. I did not know Ernie had given me the watch until Mother wrote me. But it is a lovely watch and I love it. It keeps wonderful time, too.

I have so far received no Christmas packages from home and only one card from the family, so I still have a lot to come. I got two lovely packages of good soap, toilet water and pajamas and odds and ends from Goldie. She has been swell. The Sunday school sent a grand box of homemade cookies and peanuts. It was a delicious box. Aunt Ruth sent me a nice box, also her mother. Packages are coming in slowly for me. Perhaps I'll get mine when it means more to me. Right now, we have so much candy, we do not appreciate it. And Julia, I always appreciate the magazines. Send them, please, when you can.

I must stop now and get ready for chow.

I miss you so and will be so glad when the day finally comes when we can be together again and enjoy a few spots!

Much love always and may God keep you content in Him.

Love,   Al

JODOIGNE, BELGIUM

"The war had again escalated, and we were on our way by convoy to Aachen, across the Belgian border and inside Germany. We were, again, to set up the hospital. Suddenly, and very unexpectedly, our convoy was stopped and we received orders from our First Army head-quarters to go back to Jodoigne, Belgium, which was about 50 miles in Belgium. It was late at night and we could not comprehend the idea of turning back. We were used to going ahead. The next day, we learned the reason for such an order, for we were informed that the German army had penetrated the Allied lines in the Ardennes. A great battle was raging there now, in terrible weather as the snow was heavy and still falling. This was to be known later as the Battle of the Bulge. It was in this general area where the terrible Malmedy Massacre took place. The Germans actually executed a large number of Allied troops in a most inhumane manner.

So, we had to retreat – the roads were not safe and it was an extremely dangerous situation. Retreating such a distance, it did not appear likely that we would receive casualties.

We were now located in a large Normal School for Girls – a won-derful setup for both the hospital and all our personnel. We felt safe and secure there – so far behind the front. And it was so cold and snowing and we were so war-weary – this was indeed a blessing in disguise for us. We were ready to accept patients, but did not anticipate that would be the situation. And it was Christmas time! Jodoigne was a modern, but small city, so perhaps we should take advantage of it. It was now New Year's Eve and I have hesitated to include this episode, but I feel I must – as a lighter note. We had had no casualties and so we were really on a rest period, therefore, we decided that our group would celebrate the coming of the New Year. We were friendly with a great group of enlisted men who ran our Lab. It was the policy of the army to provide officers a monthly ration of good liquor and usually that included a bottle of good French champagne. There was no such provision for the enlisted men – so unfair! I always gave my ration to them as I did not drink, and saved the champagne for a special occasion – such as peace!

On New Year's Eve, six of the nurses, including me, went to the Lab, which was on the floor above us, to celebrate. They all knew that I did not drink, so they offered me a glass of lemonade made from the lemon powder that came in our K-ration – and it really was quite good. As I was thirsty, I had two glasses of this – eight-ounce glasses – then decided to join them in a glass of champagne to greet the New Year. That was a total of three eight-ounce glasses. I was so naïve! I cannot now believe it. Very soon, I began to feel the effects and realized what must have happened. But they were my friends! I was so light headed, I knew I had to find my bed. So, I "floated" down the stairway and somehow found my cot – climbed into my sleeping bag – clothes and all – and awakened on New Year's Day with a full-blown hangover! I could not raise my head and did not leave my bed until much later in the day. My good friends in the Lab got such a kick out of it – for they knew that the lemonade was mixed – not with water – but 100 proof laboratory alcohol which has no taste, but what a kick it had! Some good friends! Happy New Year!

The general in charge of our First Army – General John Rogers – came to Jodoigne on January 2nd to present the Bronze Star to several of our medical officers and me. This was a total surprise. They assembled our entire unit outside in the snowy courtyard for the ceremony. General Rogers pinned the ribbon on my uniform and offered his congratulations. Quite a proud moment for me.

Briefly, the commendation read, "for meritorious service in connection with military operations against the enemy – as Surgical Supervisor of the 45th Evacuation Hospital in England, France and Belgium. She efficiently organized the O.R. personnel and expertly supervised their instructions during the preparatory phase for operations on the continent. In France and Belgium, she quickly adapted surgical facilities of the hospital to the needs of the patients, and she frequently remained on duty for long periods of time to bring expert nursing care and attention to battle casualties. By her untiring devotion to duty and marked nursing ability, Lt. Matthews set an example worthy of emulation." (They were writing about me!)

We remained in Jodoigne for two lovely weeks and never received any patients – so it was a wonderful period of leisure that we really needed."

January 3, 1945   Belgium

Dear Mother and All,

Well, as you have perhaps already read the enclosed paper, you know I have been awarded the Bronze Star. I received it yesterday afternoon with several other officers. General Rogers, First Army Surgeon, presented them in quite a ceremony. It was held out of doors in a lovely courtyard of the Normal School where we now are located. I know you will be proud of it and I guess I really ought to be. It is nice to know when you work hard and try to do a good job, that others realize this. Do not misunderstand me. I do what I do because I want to and really like it, but it does help when others know you are trying to do your job well. Anyway, here is the citation and, as yet, I have only received the ribbon and not the medal. I will send it on when I do receive it.

You will be glad to hear that we have moved back quite a distance where there is quiet and stillness and safety all day. Personally, I hate to move to the rear, but we had to for a period of rest. We are in a lovely, big, girls' Normal School and have quite a good hospital set-up. I only hope we stay here for a while.

I must drop Julia a line, so I will say good night and may this New Year bring peace to us all and a safe journey home. Take care of yourselves – all of you – and may God bless you.

Love to all,   Alice

A proud moment for me! Two of us were "pinned" that day. Chuck well is the other nurse

I was in charge of our Operating Room during our time in the European Theatre (ETO)

THE BERWYN POST

L. 2—No. 11   BERWYN, PENNSYLVANIA

A letter I'll always prize!

FEBRUARY, 1945

Lt. Alice Matthews Awarded Bronze Star

First Lieutenant Alice J. Matthews, 26, of 203 Monument Ave., Malvern, supervisor of surgery in an evacuation hospital in Belgium, has been awarded the Bronze Star for meritorious service with the Army Nurse Corps in England, France and Belgium from November 24, 1943, to November 1, 1944.

Lt. Matthews was cited for having "efficiently organized the operating room personnel and expertly supervising their instruction" while the unit was in England, and in France and Belgium she "quickly adapted surgical facilities to the needs of the patients and frequently remained on duty long periods of time to bring expert nursing care to the casualties."

Lt. Matthews enlisted in June, 1943, and has been overseas 14 months. She is a graduate of T-E High and the Chester County Hospital School of Nursing. A sister, Julia, is an Ensign in the Navy Nurse Corps at Bethesda, Md. and a brother, John, A. O. M. 3/c, is serving with our Navy in the Pacific.

From Berwyn Post (I went to High School in Berwyn)

Alice awarded Bronze Star

HEADQUARTERS
FIRST UNITED STATES ARMY
APO 230

200.6-Matthews, Alice J. (A)

SUBJECT: Award of Bronze Star Medal.

TO: First Lieutenant Alice J. Matthews, N-724579,
        Army Nurse Corps, United States Army.

Under the provisions of Army Regulations 600-45, as amended, you are awarded a Bronze Star Medal for meritorious service as set forth in the following:

CITATION

First Lieutenant Alice J. Matthews, N-724579, Army Nurse Corps, United States Army. For meritorious service in connection with military operations against the enemy as Surgical Supervisor, 45th Evacuation Hospital, Semimobile, from 24 November 1943 to 1 November 1944, in England, France and Belgium. First Lieutenant Matthews efficiently organized the operating room personnel and expertly supervised their instruction during the hospital's preparatory phase for operations upon the continent. In France and Belgium, she quickly adapted surgical facilities of the hospital to the needs of the patients and frequently remained on duty for long periods of time to bring expert medical care and attention to battle casualties. By her untiring devotion to duty and marked nursing ability, First Lieutenant Matthews set an example worthy of emulation. Entered military service from Pennsylvania.

COURTNEY H. HODGES
Lieutenant General, U. S. Army,
Commanding.

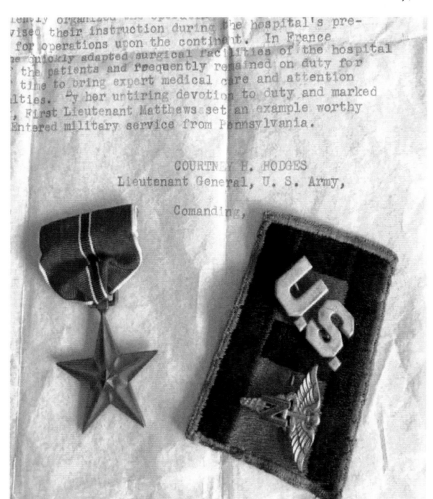

Alice's Bronze Star

SPA, BELGIUM

January 4, 1945   Belgium

Dearest Julia,

    I finally had a letter from you yesterday evening and oh, I was glad to hear from you. I miss your letters so when you do not write often. It is frequently several weeks between your letters. Your last letter was dated December 19th, so that really was delivered in very good time.

    I realize how you must feel reading in the papers all about this German counterattack and push back. But if you only could know we are back in an area of safety now, having been back there a few weeks after the push started. It was no fun, but we are way back now, enjoying peace and quiet, much as I hated to go back. I only wish we had had some way of letting Mother and the folks know I was safe and sound. News has been far from favorable in the paper and over the radio and I would give a lot just to be able to tell Mother all was okay. It is so much harder on her than it ever could be on me. Let us just hope and pray that it will all be over soon and we shall all be together in safety again.

    I guess Mother has already told you about me being awarded the Bronze Star along with several other officers and two nurses. I sent the citation on home to her to keep. It was quite a ceremony – out in the courtyard of the college. General Rogers was there to pin our ribbon on us and read the citation.

    I am sending you a lovely compact I was able to buy in this town. I think you will like it if you ever receive it. It is red leather and zipped and has hand-stitching around it. I liked it right away. I also got Frances a red leather one, only hers is square and no zipper. I finally broke down and got myself a souvenir – the first I bought overseas. I got a lovely bracelet chain and some city crest of Belgium for charms. I shall try to collect souvenir charms from here on and so I should have a nice collection by the time I get home. I only wish I had started sooner.

Take care of yourself, dear and do try to write often. If only you realized how I long for your letters. I try to write you as often as I have the time and opportunity. Be good and write.

Love always to you,   Al

January 14, 1945   Belgium

Dear Mother and All,

It is such a beautiful night - a new moon and stars galore and a new fallen snow. On the surrounding hills, we can see the dense black trees, partially covered with the snow. It is really beautiful here. We made a long move today and are now settled and quite warm and comfortable. But it took quite a lot of work to get that way. First, we took the soapy water and a broom and scrubbed the tile floor and really got results, too. And with eleven of us to a room and all our earthly belongings, we have just enough room. We have a nice pot-bellied stove to give us heat and on which we can make tea, soup or toast. It really is fun to set up in a new place - when it has such possibilities. We have a table and on it, we all pool our food stuffs together and it really is quite a store. One of the girls has a radio, so we are really quite at home. And our mess will be served to us by Belgian waitresses and cooked by Belgians so that will be quite a change for us.

Last night, I had the oddest dream. In the very middle of a battle which took place in the States, for some reason, there was a terrific change in the sky and earth and as plain as could be, I knew it was the Second Coming. I was so happy and we all started ascending to heaven and all the earth was just blotted out. Then, I woke up, but I remembered that dream – which is odd for me to do.

Please do not worry about me. I am fine. But I would like some colored wash clothes – for white ones are impossible, also pajamas – cotton or rayon.

Love to All,   Alice

"We have had some very unusual hospital locations – and we have been very versatile – but there has been none to equal this one. We were on a former German Calvary Post – a very large brick complex – large enough for two evacuation hospitals – and all the personnel. Every effort was always made to find decent buildings for use as a hospital, especially in the winter, for the winters in Germany were harsh. It was now snowing heavily and it was so beautiful.

But stables for a hospital? Would we be able to rid the buildings that we were to use for our surgery of that animal smell? And what about the building in which we were to live? It was possible, for we succeeded. We had to scrub out the stables ourselves and finally that "horsey" odor left. Now we were comfortably situated in a large room – there were eleven of us – and it was crowded – but we were warm and dry. Everything was complete – even cozy – down to our "friend" the pot-bellied stove. We used it for our heat, heating our bath water and water for tea and soup – and even for making toast. We really treasured that old "friend."

Our O.R. was well located in former horse stables – actually quite a satisfactory arrangement. We had the complete hospital set up and ready to received casualties in less than eight hours from our time of arrival. It was hard, dirty work, but with the wonderful team effort and good basic plan, even though no two set-ups were similar, we were now ready to fully function. I had now to go on duty for twelve more hours of night shift – I knew I would sleep the next day! We worked in 12-hour shifts – alternating on a fair basis, but we all had to work together to set up the hospital when we arrived in the new area. Therefore, half of our personnel of necessity would work 24 hours before going off duty. It was our way of life, and we knew it, and never questioned it.

This hospital set up here only lasted two weeks! We then moved to enjoy a rest period at Spa, Belgium, which was a famous resort town noted for its mineral baths. People used to come here from all over Europe for the healing waters. Note: Part of my responsibilities was to keep a written log of all of our surgical cases. I had just totaled them and found the total to be 8,000 cases since June 16, 1944 (It was now February, 1945. No wonder we were weary!)

The two weeks we spent in the stables had been very busy and now we were to have a two-week period of rest. The powers that be realized that the human body had its limitations – setting up a complete hospital, working long, hard hours – and days – and nights – under very difficult conditions – not only physically, but emotionally. We could become accustomed to the physical drain, for we were young and healthy. But emotionally, it was very hard to see these fine, young men – at their prime – come into surgery broken and disfigured – or even worse. This all takes place so close to the battlefield, for we were always "up there", and our casualties came directly to us from First Aid Stations. It was no wonder we were feeling the stress of our daily work."

January 20, 1945   Belgium

Dearest Mother and All,

Good morning, folks. Here I sit, snug and comfortable and really nothing to do all day, except write or read or even sleep! We are working, but are not busy yet. For the weather is awful – snowy and cold. Just the sort of weather you want to curl up in front of a warm fire – preferably an open log fire. But I am being satisfied, for the present, anyway, to substitute on old fashioned pot-bellied stove with a good coal fire in it. The kind that you roast by when you are on top of it and practically freeze by when your bed is on the opposite side of the room! But we love the old thing! And it serves us so many purposes. Mainly, of course, it heats our room and our bath water and by it we dry our clothes. But I guess the thing we all like best about it is its cooking potential! For example, I was on duty last night and since we were not doing a thing, I came off and went to bed at three. So, I did not bother going out to breakfast this morning. One of the girls brought us back coffee, bread and butter. So, we, or rather I, for I still take over when it comes to any cooking – heated the coffee, made hot toast – buttered - and Vicky had a can of bacon sent from home, which I fried. So, of course, we had to have some fried bread, too. We just couldn't waste such lovely bacon fat. Nice and crisp and brown. Now what better breakfast would anyone want! And cooked in our pot-bellied stove, too!

Of course, it had its daily interruptions. We have civilian men to clean and keep the fires going here and always when you are least presentable, they have to come along to fill the coal box, empty the dishes or sweep the room! And usually, it's in the midst of a bath! And try to make them understand what we are trying to say! Utter bedlam! So, in the very middle of our breakfast in, they come to clean the room! And spill the lovely bacon fat I was saving all over the floor! Can't you picture that mess? We are willing to clean our own room to keep them out.

I got the lovely tan socks you made for me yesterday. They will be very good for this winter snow. They are certainly nicely done, too.

Vicky was very fortunate last week, for Warren, her fiancé whom she had not seen for over fourteen months, came over to see her on a three-day pass. She was indeed a happy girl. He was in the outfit that held Bastogne for nine days after they were completely cut off after the counterattack. It was quite an unforgettable experience they had there.

Mail has been slow in coming since the attack, but I guess it will soon start on its way again. I surely hope all so, for it is quite a while since I heard from home. I just hope all is well with you. I know you write, all of you, and I do write as often as I can so eventually, we will hear. Give everyone my love – and Ruthie, this letter is for you, too.

God bless you all and keep you safe.

Love always,   Alice

January 20, 1945   Belgium

Dearest Julia,

Today is Sunday and what a lovely, peaceful Sunday, too. We have had quite heavy snows for over a week and all around it is so white, with the black trees on the hillside all around us. Just like the pictures we used to have in our geography books at school of Switzerland and Germany. And the sun is glistening on the snow, or I guess I ought to say the snow is glistening in the sun! Anyway, it is a beautiful day. I just came back from church service. We have a combined service now with another evac hospital that is located in the area.

And as for our living quarters. This time, there are eleven of us living in one room – with all our earthly belongings, in a room just a little larger than our living room at home. It is completely filled with duffle bags and clothes and the walls are lined with nails from which our respective garments hang. And our color scheme as usual is olive drab with a khaki contrast. Indeed, it is all very primitive, but we do manage to keep pretty comfortable for we have quite a congenial group in our room.

Yesterday, Goldie sent me the prettiest woolen house coat I have yet seen. Julia, it is lovely. A tailored one in a lovely blue and pink plaid pattern- very soft colors, so it really is not a conspicuous one at all – soft and warm and feminine. I love it and almost feel it is too nice to be wasted here, but I feel feminine again when I wear it. She has indeed been so good to me always. She is one grand person and a rare friend.

I am now on nights, so I'd better say cheerio and take a few winks. Write soon and

All my love,   Al

January 24, 1945   Belgium

Dearest Julia,

I received your lovely package yesterday – the one with the identification bracelet in it. Julia, it is really a beauty. I love it – it is such a good looking one and the chain is so pretty. I wish I could tell you how I really appreciate it. And all the other packages you wrapped so pretty – the cookies, nuts and chocolate syrup. All I needed was the ice cream to make a perfect chocolate nut sundae!

Things are quiet right now. It is 5:00 a.m. and only three more hours before we go off duty. Last night, we were really busy. To give you a little idea, I can tell you that we did sixty-four cases in our twelve-hour period, running six tables. And naturally, they were not small cases. We were so tired this morning, we fell into bed and slept through everything until five o'clock. We tire so much quicker now than we used to, which I guess is not hard to understand. But I do much prefer to be really busy than try to put in the time.

I wish I could make Mother understand that I am alright. I just wish she did not worry as I know she must. She wrote in her last letter enough to let me know she is going through a lot. I wish she did not have to. We naturally have our rough spats, but on the whole, have been pretty safe.

Julia, do enjoy yourself there and do not stick your neck out for overseas. It would be the same practically for you here as you have now. Only the forward hospitals really have experiences as we do. Your only difference would be that you cannot get home. So, take my advice.

I must write Mother a note, so until I write again – good night and may God bless and keep you.

My love always,   Al

Please send me something sweet.

February 2, 1945   Belgium

Dearest Julia,

One more night of night duty and then I am on day duty for two weeks. We are trying out every two weeks – alternating. Personally, I would like at least three weeks of each. But not knowing how long we may stay set here, we have to have some plan, instead of changing every time we moved, as we had formerly done. For the past three nights, I have had to go on as supervisor over the hospital and I much prefer to stay on my job in surgery. There is not an earthly thing to do, except get a report from each ward and see that all goes well. I do not like an office job anyway. I like action and plenty of it.

I had a v-mail from Aunt Ann today and she wrote that she had heard from you and you had not heard from me for six weeks! It is only on account of the mail service, I can assure you, for I always do write to you weekly anyway. I hope you realize that. No matter how busy we are or how tired I am, I do take the time out to write Mother and you. I wrote you a long letter only five days ago. Your last letter I received was written and mailed on January 4, on pretty gray air mail stationary. Pretty, yes, but you sure can use three sheets of it and say so little. It is too small

I am wondering as I write this, if you have received any orders to leave for a new station. I always look at your address to see where you write it from.

I saw in an army nursing paper that the nurses who were in England had been returned to the States. Many nurses I should have said. Short stay for them. Have you heard from Mim since they returned?

I called you recently – today in fact. And I would like to know how long it takes to get to you. I never could find out.

Can you find out from Fran if I made arrangements for her to see that Mother got flowers from me, preferably roses, on her birthday and on Mothers' Day, and some flowers for Easter? I write early for this, for I do not want it forgotten or missed due to mail irregularities. I shall enclose cards for each and you be sure to tell her to make the arrangements with Bissett and pay him for me from my account.

It is quiet here now. I guess the front is really moving forward now that the snow has stopped and nights are clear. Did I tell you our total number of operations since we came over on D-10 'til yesterday was eight thousand cases! Quite a number, eh? And it represents a lot of work too.

Well, dear, write soon and often and may we soon be together again for good.

Love always,   Al

February 5, 1045   Belgium

Dearest Mother and All,

I am really receiving the letters and boxes you have sent me. I hear from home often now and it is so good to hear from you! It makes all the difference in the world when I get mail - especially mail from home and Julia. I guess I still have a lot of back mail to come, but I am satisfied with what I am getting. Your last letter, which I got last night, was written on January 11th, so that is really quite good when you consider everything. I also got one from Frances, Eddie, Julia and a card and note from Ruthie's sister, which was certainly sweet of her. I also got the two boxes you sent in which there were some snuggies. Thanks so much. I really do not need them while we are in buildings, but when we go out in the field again, they will be most welcome.

Several hours later

I had to stop to take my daily bath and a few chores and get my mail. We pick it up every day around six and today I got another package from you. It had peanut butter and crackers, peach jam and soup and Kleenex in it. It really was a nice package and I shall add it to our larder or perhaps I shall take the jelly and peanut butter down to our snack bar in surgery. I keep a pitcher of coffee and one of chocolate and crackers there all day long for our personnel. And they certainly do enjoy it after operating so constantly - going from one case to another - they really need that pick-up in between.

I am now on day duty so, naturally we have to have a rainy spell. We had such a very heavy snow for several weeks. We thought it would be weeks before it would disappear and then we had one very rainy day and - kaput- all the snow was gone. And now it feels like spring out - balmy breezes.

Eddie, we were stationed at Eupen (look it up on you map) and that was our home for four months, so you see how close we were to Aachen during the whole attack on the city. Then, after the counterattack, we moved way back into Jodoigne, and that was when I had the chance to go to Brussels. Of course, I cannot tell you where I am now, but you have a pretty good idea from your letter. In fact, you guessed within a few miles. But it is very quiet here now as our troops have naturally advanced. I did appreciate your letter – you are really a wit, my dear. But I am afraid you will be really a man, when I see you again!

I am answering all three of your letters in this one, so please realize I am trying to write all of you.

So, you are making a scrap book of my souvenirs, etc. I must try to send a few different things home. I am glad you are doing it for me for I have often felt I would like to make one of my army days, I ought to say years, for it is almost four now. But I just didn't have the right time to do it. Thanks for doing it for me. The only thing I am going to request from you personally, is to send me magazines – especially Redbook and Cosmopolitan, as I rarely see them. Our girls get several others, but not those or Good Housekeeping. Let me know if you need a request and I'll send it to you every month.

I am sorry I have not mentioned receiving your stamps Mother, but I have, in many different letters and I do appreciate them so much. Apparently, I have written you letters you never got, for I wrote you telling I got the six pair of pants and also the sox you knit and both are so useful.

How I'd love to spend a few quiet evenings at home, but if I had a chance for a leave to the States. I doubt if I would want to go until this is all over. I couldn't go through leaving home again and knowing what was ahead. When I go home, I want to stay there.

Well, I must do some necessary jobs before I go to bed, so I will say goodnight to all of you and may God bless all of you – Mother, Ernie, Fran and Eddie and of course Ruthie. Write often and I'll do the same.

Love always,   Alice

February 7, 1945   Belgium

Dearest Julia,

We have been so busy. I guess we never realized fully how you folks back home must have worried during the great German counter-attack. But now that it is all a thing of the past and we can look back on it, we realize how much worry it must have caused everyone back there who had any of their family in the area.

Bad and although that was, we were talking today of how busy we used to be when we first came over to France, for the first few months it was a real hell. Our wards were always full to over-capacity and surgery ran one horrible mutilated case through after the other. You would never believe it unless you could have walked through our pre-operative and shock wards and had seen what was there. And now unless there is a big push on, our casualties are comparatively light. Oh, we will get in some bad cases from mines, etc., but the Germans have not had the chance to lay the mines as they used to. I guess the final push will be like our first months were. But may it not last as long!

For four days now, they have threatened us with General Hawley, the chief surgeon of the E.T.O. He is supposed to visit us and have a general inspection. Each day we would get things all spic and span and then only a full colonel and a one-star general would make an appearance. So, today he finally came, and of course, just walked on through – after looking at a case that was going on. Do you have to report and salute to any superior officer when they come around? We do and you feel like a fool when you do it. Outside, you do not mind saluting, but inside, it seems so ridiculous. I hate all the fuss they make over rank in the Army. But I guess the Navy is just the same.

I am glad you are fixing up a scrapbook for me. I always wanted to fix it, but somehow never had a decent chance or adequate interest. It will be a nice thing to look at and reminisce over when I get back home. I'll try to send some more souvenirs that can be used in a scrap book.

Julia, you sound as if you think we have a chance of being relieved of duty in the near future. I think you can remove all such ideas from your mind – for I can assure you – unless a miracle happens, we stay here until the end, then stand a fair chance of seeing duty in another theater – namely China, Burma and India area. Doesn't that sound encouraging? Naturally, I never mention the idea to Mother, so I trust you will not say a thing. I guess First Army has made too good a reputation for their own good! So next time I see you, I may have false teeth and gray hair, but please do not let me see you notice the change – I may be quite sensitive in my old age!

Keep writing often, dear, and I shall keep you posted to the best of my ability.

Love always, Al

February 9, 1945   Belgium

Dearest Mother and All,

Today, I am sitting here in a small "parfumier" shop in this town and patiently waiting for a permanent – which I still hope to get. I need one badly and it is the only way to have your hair – short and curled! But they are so slow here and have to stop and talk using their hands the way the French do. But we are going into another building tomorrow, so I have a free afternoon. We went into a little restaurant and there sat a soldier with four full sized pies in front of his place and he had a whole one in his hand and was eating that. Said he, "I'm hungry. They do not feed you very well up front!" Two of them were going to eat all of those pies!

Just a note – that is all this passes for.

With all my love,   Alice

"Once again, I must tell you about our Pudgy. She presented us with yet another litter of puppies. We cannot tell what nationality they were – but Pudgy must be breaking all rules and fraternizing!"

Mascot "Pudgy" and another litter

February 11, 1945   Belgium

Dearest Mother and All,

Sunday – a warm fire and a rest period again. For some reason, they are killing us with kindness of late. But we love it really!
We only worked for two weeks this time and now we again are on an
indefinite period of rest. And what a set-up! Yesterday, we moved out
of our stable-hospital into what used to be a small private sanitarium
– just our officers and commanding officer and executive officer. It
is about two miles out of the town and way off by itself. Really, it is
quite modern and a very beautiful home. There are eight in our room,
and really, it is not too crowded. A lovely, modern home with a lot of
built-in closets and drawers and shelves and two lovely large windows with lovely drapes. If we only had the where-with all - we have a
nice balcony opening off our room. And steam heat! And not least of

123

all, there is a huge, modern bathroom opening off our room – lovely and white and maroon tile and a lovely, big white tub! We are all so anxious to try it out, but – no hot water until tomorrow! What a treat to take a real tub bath again! Many long months since our last one. All of the floors are either a lovely tile or all inlaid hardwood and the rooms downstairs are all beautifully paneled – ceilings in dark beams and pale pink plaster. And we use the original living room as such – having several lovely, comfortable chairs and a huge overstuffed sofa that easily seats six and tables and a radio we brought along. A fireplace with a coal grate, helps to make the room more homey. We eat in the dining room, oddly enough, and have Belgian waitresses and cooks and excellent food. It is so like a dream after all that has gone on before, and we are enjoying every minute of it. Fresh eggs for breakfast and fresh oranges for dinner. So, knowing all this, you can relax and stop worrying about me.

And to top it all off, day before yesterday, I went into the town and got a lovely permanent. What must be equal to a cold-wave at home. It is so safe and natural and no frizz at all – and all for 250 francs (about six dollars)! By the time I return home, I wonder if I shall recall our own monetary system! English, French, Belgium and German – I hope our next dealings can be in dollars and dimes!

As for the forty dollars I had been sending, I always wrote and told you when I was not going to send it on. From now on, I am not going to send it as far as I know. I am going to keep it out, for so many things turn up and I hate to borrow. So, just do not bother with any more bonds. Take my church money out of the other, and when I can, I shall send any other money.

Julia writes often lately, and I am now wondering if perhaps she has moved. I wonder where she will go after she leaves Bethesda? She is one girl who will really miss her trips home! Not that I didn't, but it has been so long and all my years of service (sound like an old army man, eh?) were so far away from home.

Well, I will write again soon, if our rest period continues. I only hope and trust God, that all goes well at home and my thoughts are ever with you folks at home – for that is where I would love to be.

Keep writing and may God be with each and every one of you always.

Love,   Alice

"We had an interesting experience when we made a visit to a farm near our unit, investigating all the barking we had been hearing. We found it was coming from some beautiful "husky dogs", the sled dogs like the ones they used in Alaska, but these came from Greenland. This had been such a hard winter – heavy snows and still more predicted. So, the Army flew eighty-one of these dogs – nine teams with nine dogs on each team – for the purpose of transporting supplies and the wounded from the front line. A pipe dream really – it was so impractical. Ironically, as soon as the dogs arrived, the snow melted and was replaced by mud!

Such handsome animals! They loved attention and affection, but they were out of their element here. They were well cared for and exercised daily – hitched to a jeep without a motor which the dog team pulled on the road. They treated two of us to a most unusual ride – using "dog power" in place of "horse power." The way they responded to the instructions their trainer called to them was unbelievable. They knew each command and obeyed at once. I do hope they were returned to the cold climate."

Alice and Nurse Nolan go for a Husky powered ride

February 25, 1945   Belgium

Dear Mother and All,

It is now time for church, but today I am going to write to you instead. I felt I'd rather take the half hour out and write you. For odd as it may seem to you, and odder as it is to me, in spite of this tremendous push of yesterday, four of us are going to Paris tomorrow for a three-day pass. It is almost unbelievable that we are, in the view of recent events, on the front – but I for one will surely not question it! I am going with Nolan and she is quite excited for plenty of reason. She is going to see her sister, who is a WAC and she is just recently stationed in Paris! And she hasn't seen her for two years! She has been in Africa and Italy with the WACs. And since Gertie last saw her, she, her sister, was married. So, it will be quite a reunion for them.

But we did not see much of Paris itself when we were there before, since that was only four days after it was liberated. This time, we will try to see Notre Dame, too. For we shall have three full days there as our travel time is not included. We are very fortunate that one of the girls going is the "friend" of the First Army executive officer of the surgeon's office. So, for that reason, we have a regular staff sedan to travel in – a real civilian car instead of a big truck. We shall make the trip all in one day. It is about three hundred miles and in comfort. I never expected to get back to Paris – especially after this big offensive, but we are almost on our way!

I will try to write you from Paris. We stay at a lovely hotel the army has taken over.

Take care of yourself and God bless you all.

Love in haste,   Alice

ESCHWEILER, GERMANY

"We had a wonderful time in Paris – seeing so many places of interest and importance. It was a great experience and we felt so lucky to have this unexpected trip. When we returned from our trip, we were sorry to hear that our Chief Nurse – Capt. McLin – was to be promoted to Chief Nurse of the 15th Army – as major. We were happy for her, but we would miss her as we had been through so many experiences together – and she always stood firmly by her nurses."

After three wonderful weeks of rest, we were anxious to return to our work. The Allies were starting a big push into Germany, and now we have received our orders to move forward to the small German village of Eschweiler."

"There had been heavy bombing in this area and we were to set up our hospital in an older civilian hospital – and it certainly did not look very promising. It had been bombed, nearly all the windows were out, and we would have had a better set up using our tents! But we did not have the choice, so we all went to work cleaning up the mess inside. There was so much trash and debris every place, we just threw it out the windows – to join all the rubble already out there. It was surprising how much hard work and soap and water – and teamwork can accomplish. Fortunately, we had had a good rest and were ready to take on this challenge. Really had pretty good results for our efforts."

March 8, 1945   Germany

Dearest Julia,

I hope you understand that we have been busy – and I have not written you since before I went to Paris. Look at my home address and then you will see the reason for it. We finally made it across the boundary after "sweating it out" on the Belgium border for over four months. I really have so much I ought to write you, since I have been to Paris and all. I will start anyway.

We had a lovely time in the gay city - saw all the places of interest on a sight-seeing tour. And we had lovely quarters in one of the hotels. It is now a nurses' quarters for nurses on leave. And the rooms are lovely - connecting bath and clean sheets on a lovely innerspring mattress! Meals served in a lovely dining room and a snack bar where you could buy coffee and doughnuts any hour of the day. We went shopping. You really can buy very little, for the articles for sale are really luxury items at a tremendous price. I did get two perfumes. I am going to save them, for what, I have no idea. I got a little silver Notre Dame and Eiffel Tower for my charm bracelet, too. Coming back in the car, I had the rare treat of driving for over eighty miles - from Reims to Dinant - quite a stretch of road, too. It was so good to get behind the wheel of a car again!

And now we are back on the job again. Our rest period was too long, for we went back to a full schedule and it is so hard to get used to it. Off duty, bath and to bed and you are aching all over - you are so tired. I do not like so long a rest. A week is wonderful, but three weeks of doing nothing is too much for me.

We are in a former civilian hospital and what a dirty hole it was! We have to start from scratch and clean up the whole place before we can start to set up our own hospital. Junk was piled up high all over the place. We are now fully set up and have been for several days. We opened a full day after we moved in. It is a lot of hard work, for we may stay there for only a week or ten days. I have no idea. It depends on the Front. But it is a lot of work. Come civilian days, I think I could set up a hospital in anything – we have proven that.

Well, what snap did you get of me that you thought was so good? I cannot recall it. I am still waiting for more of you.

Still, no word of a change for you? I am waiting to hear, for I know you must have gotten them by now. Isn't the suspense awful?

Keep writing and real soon.

All my love,   *Al*

"Soon, the casualties began to pour in — a steady flow and once again, we were very busy. But we knew that the Allied Army was moving forward rapidly and that meant our stay at this area would not be a very long one. We were going to win this war — and soon — our spirits are really high.

Concentrating on our work and the welfare of our troops, we had given very little thought to the civilian population and what this war was doing to their lives. Most of them are certainly the victims of a terrible war."

HONNEF, GERMANY

The personnel had worked tirelessly in Eschweiler to make their hospital clean from all the debris and rubble, only to find out they were yet to move again. Their spirits were raised upon hearing that they were to cross the Rhine River. They would be the first Evac Hospital in the Army to accomplish this feat.

"The 45th Evac Hospital approached the Rhine River at Honnef, Germany. This was a very important bridgehead, and the Allied Armored division crossed just ten minutes before the Germans had planned to blow it up in March. Ten days later, the bridge collapsed into the Rhine River — weakened by the heavy traffic and the incessant bombing. But the Army Engineer Corps had soon laid a pontoon bridge across into Rhineland. When we crossed the Rhine, we were the first evacuation hospital to cross the Rhine River into Germany.

We made three stops, setting up our complete hospital, but each time we had orders to pack up and move forward as the front was advancing so rapidly. We then received definite orders to go forward about two hundred miles from Eschweiler to a very beautiful spot — Bad Wildungen. We did not know it at this time, but it was to be our most ideal location."

March 30, 1945   Germany

Dearest Julia,

For one half hour, I have been standing here, looking out my window, at people passing by. It really is fascinating. First, they have their head line, and I certainly mean line! It seems as if the entire town turns out the first thing in the morning, and stand for hours, just to get their loaves of very dark brown bread. No wonder they call it black bread when you read about it! Some of the people are very well dressed and look as if war has not touched them, whereas others really show it. Then, after the folks have gotten their ration of bread, they return to their homes and in a very short time, you see the parade all over again, only this time they are all carrying a container of every size and description and most of them pushing or pulling a cart or even a baby carriage with a very large container in it. Some of the carts are big enough to have a horse in front of it. And instead, you see a little old lady pulling sometimes with help, sometimes alone. These folks are on their way to get their water supply for the day. The only source of water in this town now is the river. So, you see them going and then in an hour or so, they return with their full load. Their next time out is to do what little marketing they can. So, it is a very full morning for them. But I have noticed what a very clean place this is. In the early morning, they are out sweeping the street in front of the house! You just do not see any dirt or refuse.

It is really very beautiful around here. I can look out my window and see a beautiful scene of hill after hill – little houses snuggled in the valleys and on the hillside and all the trees and bushes are just starting to bloom and blossom. It seems utterly impossible that war is going on – until you look out and observe more closely at the buildings and see in the roof of the civilian hospital next to us where either a shell of a bomb has made a huge hole and also that all the windows of this place, and many others, are completely out or broken. In going through all the towns that really took the brunt of the battles, such as Aachen and Duren, and around the bridgehead at Remagen, you wonder how there ever will be a city there again. They are absolutely and completely in ruins. And you can easily realize how much post-war construction there will be to do. Germany and France will have to be completely built up. They will indeed be modern countries after the war!

Isn't the war news too good to be true! We are all so excited and listen to all the news we can. It just can't possibly last too much longer. Of course, this war will not seem to be over as far as we are concerned, until we are all home. And if only we were sure of being home six months after war is over. But we certainly are not. The C.B.I. and army of occupation stare us in the face. But perhaps they will change things and send us back. Everything is uncertain and only time will tell. It doesn't seem possible that after all these years of war, that it soon may end.

I am anxious to hear from you and to hear the news from you and home. I do hope Johnny and Ruthie got married.

I got the box of Hersey bars from you day before yesterday. It certainly was sweet of you. Thanks a million.

Well, I must turn in now, so do write when you can and I'll do so also.

Much love always,   Alice

"The war news was so encouraging – all reports that came back to us indicated this war could not last too much longer. But then we began to hear the disturbing news that following this phase of the war, there was a very real possibility that we would either be kept in Europe as part of the occupation army – or even worse – be sent to the other war area now called the C.B.I. (China – Burma – India). We would not dwell on that now – for now we must concentrate on getting this war behind us victoriously."

BAD WILDUNGEN, GERMANY

"We arrived in this most idyllic spot totally unprepared for its natural splendor. It was located in the very mountainous area – heavily forested and breathtakingly beautiful. There was no outward evidence of the war, until we realized this was an 'open or neutral zone' – for just across the road and up the mountain, the Germans had set up convalescent hospitals! This was an eye-opener and so difficult for us to comprehend. All around us were Germans in uniform – free to come and go. They were all so friendly and so helpful to us. Before we arrived, they had sent staff over to our hotel to clean and prepare our area for our arrival. And a group of German medical officers came over to welcome us when we arrived. C'est la guerre!

Bad Wildungen was a resort area – used by the theatrical and screen stars and often referred to as the 'Hollywood of Germany', for that reason only, no other comparison applies. Our 'home' here was a magnificent luxury hotel in a heavily wooded area at the base of a mountain. How wonderful that would be."

April 6, 1945   Germany

Dearest Mother and All,

I'm afraid I must have seemed to have been neglecting you this past week, for I have not had time to write at all. We have made another move - quite a lengthy one and are very busy here. I am still on nights and have been just dying once I get to bed in the morning. Today, I got up a little early, for I just had to drop you a note. All the way here, and since we have been here, I have thought of so many interesting things I could write to you about. And if we were not busy, you would have an interesting letter. But if I recall all I wanted to say later, I will write it as soon as we slacken, if we do. I will say we are in a lovely town - a former resort town in a beautiful hotel. I have quite a few post cards and pamphlets of the place that I can send on later. They are in English!

We are very comfortable here – three to a room – minus the real furniture, of course. Only our C.O. and Chief Nurse can rate that! C'est la guerre! But we have running water and johns that flush – two luxuries indeed. And heat in our radiators. It is our nicest set-up yet. So much nicer than tents! Especially when I look at and see the rain! But we have made so many moves in the past three weeks, with complete hospital set-ups each time. Everyone is worn out, especially the boys, for they have so many boxes and tables and such to load and unload. It is no cinch for them. I just hope we stay here a few months. There are several large German hospitals here for convalescent soldiers (Jerry) for this town is our open one. It is odd to see your enemy walking around free as the air – in complete uniform! We were practically greeted by two Jerry captains in full uniform when we came here. They had a detail of convalescent soldiers to clean up the hotel before we got in. It is a funny war we are fighting – in many more ways than one.

But do not worry about me, since this is a medical center, we are perfectly safe here.

I am very anxious to hear the home front news. Our mail has been delayed since we moved and we sure miss it. I did get two packages from you the day we left Honnef, our last area. I can mention that since it is so far back - fruit cake and candy and soup and underwear. It was swell. We are eating the fruitcake now.

I will write soon again and tell you all I can.

Take care of yourself and love to all.

Love always,   Alice

"We were busy – receiving and operating on 60-80 cases every twelve hours – using twelve operating tables all the time – our maximum capacity. We all realized that we were reaching our limits. After a full year of war, the physical and emotional drain was becoming evident on each of us – although we truly did not fully realize this was so. We loved our work, but did wonder how long we could continue at such a pace. Of course, we all knew we would find reserve resources within each of us as needed. And the war news was constantly getting more optimistic."

April 10, 1945   Germany

Dearest Julia,

I finally am going to make myself take time out to write a halfway decent letter to you. Just realize, if you can, that I have been too tired to write and that is something coming from me – for I am supposed to have unlimited energy! You see, I haven't changed any! But these past two weeks have really been hard ones – full hours and trying ones. When we come off duty, we are really exhausted. I have been tired before, but I think after almost a year of it over here under this strain it is hard on you. I enjoy it though. It is hard to explain, but I like my work and O.R. personnel. And that means a lot.

We have been busier lately since the Ruhr push – more like our first day in Normandy. We run on an average of ten tables, often eleven and that is really a full-time job trying to keep everyone happy, supplies up, patients on each table and feed them. Yes – I have my snack bar and keep hot chocolate, coffee, bread, peanut butter and jelly there all night long. And there are about thirty or more that eat and drink there. So, that is a job in itself. But how they all appreciate it. In between cases, it helps them and it is no easy job for a surgeon to go right from one big case to another, and we average fifty to sixty cases a night. So, we do not fool around at all.

Right now, I have the sweetest group of litter bearers – all about nineteen and they are darling. Full of fun and good workers although they are no bigger than Eddie. They call me "Mom!" They all do now – say I take good care of them – even the doctors and visiting teams we have to help out. Guess I am too maternal, and that sure won't get me anything! Right? Right?

Well, I've had a real hot tub bath, one of the luxuries of this hotel, so I'm ready for a full day's sleep. And I will! Write real soon. All my love,   Al

April 13, 1945   Germany
Dearest Mother and All,

Tonight, I got a letter from Ernie – March 9 – and a box from home – olives, shampoo and crackers. I only wish there were some way I could let you know how I appreciate your packages. It means so much to go down for mail and see a box from home. Like a part of home coming over here to me. I haven't been requesting anything in my last letter as I hate to ask for something that is hard for you to get. I certainly do not want you to go to any trouble for the boxes, please. I mean that. If I do ask for something that is hard to get, please do not hesitate to tell me. I have been away so long that I do not know the score about such things at home now. While on the topic, there are two things I could use if you can easily buy them – only cotton socks – size 9 ½ or 10 – any color and some toilet water or cologne – any kind. I liked that Old Spice and Old South, and Apple Blossom, Lavender or anything not too sweet. I have perfume, but I am out of cologne. And please use my money for these things – I really want you to. Even if Ernie's letter was an old one, it was good to hear from home.

Ernie, I am glad you liked the cigarette case, and I wish you would not be concerned about me buying things over here. Naturally, prices are fairly high, but if you only know what pleasure I got out of the few things I do get a chance to buy and send home, you would not mention it. After all, if I were home, I would be spending a lot more on different things than I've ever spent over here. By the way, someday, would you give me an idea what I have saved up to date? I really have no idea.

The war news over here is really unbelievably good. We all try to hear all the radio reports on the front advances. And follow it on the map. Every day, we get closer to Berlin and lately it seems as if we are just racing towards it. Today, North Army is reported only sixty odd miles from Berlin and that is not far. All the roads into Berlin are excellent highways, too. Won't it be wonderful to hear news of our troops in Berlin! Perhaps, at this rate, by the time you receive this, it shall be a fact. To see an end to all of this bloodshed and slaughter does not seem possible. We have had over ten thousand cases go through our surgery and I have seen over half that number on my shift alone – and that is only one small part – one very small part of all the wounded – to say nothing of all those who never even started out to a hospital – who never had a chance. One poor fellow today, on the ward, was having such pain with his leg – a severed artery of several days ago – and we always try to save the leg – but usually it has to be amputated – and the surgeons were discussing amputating. He wanted to know how he could tell his mother. He was only 21, and if he would have a wooden one. Between pain and facing losing a leg, the poor kid could do nothing but cry. I tried to comfort him, but what could you say? I felt more like crying myself. It was his third time wounded and he was just at the end of his endurance. You see so much of that every day and that poor kid has been in my mind all day. War really and truly is hell.

I didn't plan on writing this to you at all – I just sort of wondered off into it. I know I ought not write such things at all – so forgive me.

Write soon and take care of yourself – all of you. I'll keep writing every chance I have.

Love to all of you always, Alice

April 19, 1945   Germany

Dearest Julia,

    I have had two letters from you this past week and it has been so good hearing from you. I have missed all of you so much these past few weeks. I guess it is because Johnny was home and you were all there and I was over here and had to miss the first wedding of our family. I do not think I have ever been so homesick. I guess I've had enough of all this over here. All I want now is for the war to be over – both here and in the Pacific. And while I am on the subject, I want to be very frank with you. I am quite serious when I say we that have been overseas for less than two years will not be going home when this war over here is over. That has been made quite plain to us. Even those who have been in England and never seen any combat or even field life will go home first if they have been over longer. So do not build up any false ideas of me being home. It would not at all surprise any of us to be sent to C.B.I. (China – Burma – India). Everything here is very unsettled and uncertain in regards to our status after Germany capitulates. You get so you just let the Army make all your plans for you – they will anyway. It will be so wonderful to be able to once again, make your own plans! So, you see, I have no hopes of any soon return home, even after this theater is over. If it does come, it will be a most pleasant surprise.

    And please, do not expect to see "captain" before my name. In our outfit, there is only one captain, no matter how long you have been in. Only the Chief Nurse rates a "Captain's" rating! I have been in four years now and eighteen months overseas – and ten full months on the continent.

    I certainly have not started out in a cheerful mood. Please forgive me. I did not intend to write to you like this at all.

I am glad you liked the snap I sent of Gert and me. I think it is the best I have had. The girl I go around with and have ever since our last months in England is Vicky. I'm sure I've mentioned her in some of my letters. She is the tall girl with glasses – a pretty girl. Of course, no one shall ever take the place of Goldie. She was more like a sister to me and there is only one of her in this world. Vicky and I are good friends, but it is very different than Goldie. There are seven of us that pal around together – Vicky, Brooks, Gert, Fazie, Wilson and Crim. As a rule, we all get along very well together. Vicky works with me in surgery – a good worker and very intelligent. Talking about surgery, do you know we have averaged a thousand cases a month since we have been on the continent? And that is good, for there have been several rest periods and slack periods during that time. We now have over ten thousand operations listed.

Julia, I wish you could see Germany – under different conditions, of course. But it is a really beautiful country. Why they are not satisfied to stay put and enjoy what they have, is beyond me. The section we are in is very hilly and heavily wooded, and with spring here, now it is really like a picture. At times, it is very hard to realize there is a war. I am anxious to move away from this spot, so I can send the pictures and pamphlets I have of this building and country.

I want to send along a lovely letter Ruthie wrote me after her honeymoon. She is really a lovely girl and I know they will both be happy.

Write soon, Julia, I need your letters so much now.

All my love always   Al

NOHRA, GERMANY

April 20, 1945   Germany

Dearest Mother and All,

The more I see of Germany, the more I wonder why she was not content with such a beautiful country. Day before yesterday, we went about sixty miles or more further into Germany. One of the officers had to go on business, so we went for the ride. And the country is really lovely. That is, all except the heavy damage done by our air force. The country is very densely wooded and the place all very hilly – really small mountains. The ride we took reminded me so very much of the land and drive around Valley Forge – only the hills are higher. But the woods and the stream beside the wood was so much the same. It all proves that no one is ever really satisfied with their lot, no matter how much they have. I can easily see why people used to tour Germany on hiking trips. It is ideal for that.

It was so good to hear all about the wedding and family. Naturally, it did make me more homesick than any other one thing could. But perhaps I shall be home for Eddie's wedding! When will that be, Eddie? I have had accounts of the wedding from you, Fran, Julia, Ellen and a lovely letter from Ruthie – written after she and Johnny returned from their honeymoon. She is so happy and of course, they both have every reason to be happy. I used to think the age of 18 and 21 too young for marriage, but I now often wonder if it is not the ideal age if you are in love. Then I wonder if there is any ideal age for marriage. I hope not, for if so, mine are way back in the past, I'm afraid! It doesn't seem possible that Johnny is now married – and I was not there. Somehow, I ought to have been. Wasn't it good though, that Dutch and Alan could both be there! And that Julia could get a week off! It must have been a grand family reunion indeed! I am so anxious to see some pictures. I hope they had a decent wedding photo made. I will be very disappointed if they did not. I know they made a handsome couple for they are both unusually attractive.

I am re-reading some of your letters and some from Frances, to be sure I answer all your questions, so if this letter seems disconnected, and it will, that is the reason why.

I have gotten the Kreme shampoo twice and it really is the best we have used yet. I say we, for Vicky and I use it. In this hard water, it is by far the nicest for our hair. I will appreciate more if you can easily get it. It is always welcome. As for stockings, if you can find any of a decent texture and shade, to go with O.D. clothing. Any we can get, are an awful grayish shade. And we do wear our skirts when we have any time off – it makes us remember we are still females. Sometimes, it is easy to forget it, too!

This is a crazy, fool war we are fighting. The fellows are all lectured and told repeatedly about fraternizing with German civilians. Yet, we have any number of civilians working for us every move we make and to top it all off, yesterday, several of us were standing by the front door and out comes two Nazi officials – medical men as far as I know, they wore a red cross anyway, and walk into the building as if they really belonged here. One was a full colonel and the other a general major. And one of our G.I.'s driving the car! I can tell you, it certainly gives you a funny feeling to see a Nazi in full uniform with all regalia walking around with every privilege while their men are killing ours and vice versa. I am still trying to find out the details. If I do, I shall let you know.

Tomorrow, we again change our place of abode. We hate to leave this beautiful spot, hotel and all. We know it will never be repeated, for it is so beautiful. You will understand what I mean when I send the pictures and pamphlets on to you after we leave.

I do not know if you got my letter asking for Frankie's address. I would like to have it. Did I tell you I had a letter from Georgie? He is here in Germany and I am trying to find out where he is. I would love to see him. It would be the first I've seen of any one over here. He said he did not think he was too far away. So perhaps we can make it. I surely hope so.

I knew there was something I particularly wanted to say and that is about the wedding gift – the war bond you got for Johnny and Ruthie. Please do me a favor and take enough of my money from the bank to make my share $100. I really want it that way. I make plenty and by the time I get home, I'll have enough to start out as a civilian on it. I really want it that way, so make Ernie accept it. There surely is no reason why he ought to do it alone. I'll be quite hurt if you do not do as I request.

Well, not bad for a letter, is it? I feel quite proud of myself. Just hope it finds all of you in good health and staying so.

Don't worry about me. I am fine.

Love to all always,   Alice

WEIMER, GERMANY - BUCHENWALD CONCENTRATION CAMP

"We left our "paradise", hating to leave all that beauty and peace. We advanced about 100 miles – realizing as we went forward that every mile would be taking us closer to home! (We hoped!) It had not been the original plan for this move to be a rest period, but as it developed, it had to be.

We are now learning about the infamous German concentration camps – the Death Camps – used mainly for the mass extermination of the Jews. When our C.O. found how terrible conditions were here, it was decided the nursing staff would be put on a rest period.

We were assigned a very comfortable house – quite attractive and modern. There were flowers in abundance – it was springtime – and so many beautiful tulips were in bloom. We picked armfuls of tulips and apple blossoms. We had every reason to be content and relaxed in our new home. And there were strong rumors that the nurses would receive a seven-day pass – for a trip to the French Riviera! This had to mean that this war was truly coming to an end. Please, God, may this be so!

We did go to the Riviera, and there will be more details about that beautiful interlude, but I must first address the unbelievable reality of the concentration camps – specifically Buchenwald. Just a week ago, this camp had been liberated by Allied troops and that was when everything became common knowledge.

Up to this time, we had never been aware that there were such places as concentration camps. Very soon, our education would begin. The reason we were now having a rest period was due to the fact that conditions at the camp were so indescribably horrible, that it was decided it was not a fit place for the nurses. When our colonel saw the awful conditions in the camp, with so many contagious diseases, and knowing the nurses had been through so much, he decided that the nurses should not stay in the camp. We felt the colonel was trying to protect us. We felt a bit of resentment in that decision, until we saw it for ourselves. We knew it was something new, very important and something dreadful. And we didn't shy away from dreadful things at all. We knew there was starvation and mass death. Our officers and enlisted men were there to evaluate what could – and must – be done. There was typhus, typhoid fever, malnutrition, filth, and all kinds of communicable diseases. The conditions were so awful, it was beyond human comprehension. We were soon to see this first hand, for it was thought imperative that all staff members should make a tour of the camp.

There were guided tours of Buchenwald for military and civilians. Everyone was to see the atrocities for themselves, so there could be no denial of what man had done to man. The civilians were lined up and made to go through Buchenwald, whether they wanted to or not, as they shared in the responsibility for the existence of these horror camps. Naturally, they all protested that they had no knowledge that such camps existed. There could be no question that they knew, as there were too many positive indications. Citizens could see the camps and the prisoners, wearing striped clothing, unhealthy skin, and so thin you could see backbones seen through their abdomens, going to the work sites at stone piles and munitions plant – anywhere they could do menial, heavy, dirty work. The civilians went through the camp holding their noses or with their hands over their mouths. The stench! They were Germans and this was done by Germans – their countrymen.

Following the tour of the camp, I came back to my room and wrote my family to relate to them all I had seen and heard. I had to be certain they believed it was true when it was reported in the papers at home. So, I would like to quote at length from the letter – it is much too important for people to learn the terrible facts."

April 23, 1945   Germany

145

Dearest Mother and All,

Today, I took a very short trip to hell and back. To make it a mite clearer, we went to 'visit' a German concentration camp. And I do not exaggerate when I say Hell. Unless I had seen it all with my own eyes and heard what I heard from prisoners themselves, I doubt if I would have believed it myself. To make it clearer to you, I will start at the very beginning.

Not too far from this setup, is a German concentration camp. Just a week ago, the Americans took the camp over and now conditions existing in those camps are really being brought to light. There were sixty thousand men - and children in there and the place was made to house only about one-tenth that number. That in itself would have been enough to make life most miserable.

Every allied soldier and German civilian are to be allowed to see existing conditions and encouraged to do so. The civilians declare and maintain they were absolutely unaware of what went on. But that is hard to believe. They just could not live so close to it and not have some idea.

We were taken to the camp by truck loads and when we arrived, were given a guide to show us around. The guide was an Austrian prisoner of war – a former army officer, whose father was up high in the Austrian army. He had been seven years a prisoner. Only one year here in this camp. Which, by the way, was supposed to be the most comfortable and most lenient than any concentration camp. He spoke English quite well and seemed to know what he was talking of. He showed us first one of the punishments for various acts within the camp. A prisoner was tied down, bending forward and beaten with a club - twenty-five lashes! One of the less severe forms of punishment as you shall see. I warn you, this is not a very pleasant letter and certainly serves to make us utterly hate every German existing - wrong though that is. We then went into the crematory.

It is just what it sounds like – big ovens where they burned the dead - and dying. Dying usually from starvation and mistreatment. You could still see the bones of the latest victims. The ones in command of the camp fled before they could really complete their job. It was a most horrible and nauseating sight to see. There were about ten large furnaces or really ovens with their body-sized grill on each one. The awful odor of dead flesh still permeated the room. From here, we went outside to start our tour. And what a starting place we had! Behind the crematory there was the horrible sight of one large wagon full of dead bodies and a huge pile beside it. Absolutely dead from starvation and disease. And they must have numbered some two hundred without exaggeration. And still, they were carrying out bodies as we were there. Those already there shall be buried, but in the most part, they are leaving them as they are to really impress everyone of all that went on. Each body was nothing but a little skin over bones. Something you would not believe unless you saw. They say an average of two hundred a day died there aside from those actually killed. It was an awful sight and it will take a long time, if ever, to get it out of my mind. Poor, poor fellows. What they must have gone through before the actually died or were killed!

One of the most pathetic sights I saw was the children there. Anywhere from two years up were there, but the youngest I saw was about twelve. One was thirteen - a prisoner for a year (they are taken prisoner with their parents) and he was wounded by an S.S. soldier while being transported from one place to another. Absolutely skin and bones. And no wonder. For their meals – once daily they had a piece of black bread and a bowl of watery, greasy turnip soup. Awful stuff. And that was all. Now, of course, the Americans and allies have given them food and clothing and they get more meat in one day than they were getting in four weeks before. They are absolutely overjoyed that we had taken the camp and were too happy and elated to work for several days. It is like heaven and some do not even want to leave now. Of course, most of them have no plans to go anyway. Their countries are still occupied and everything they ever had is long since gone – especially after so many years.

One Yugoslavian spoke very good English and it turned out he was from Philadelphia no less! His two sons - both born in Philadelphia, were killed in this camp. Both American citizens! For the most, the prisoners were all from European countries and political prisoners of Germany, including Germans, and of course, Jews, for no more reason than they are Jews. Then there was a total of forty American, British and Canadian fliers who came down over Germany and were finally killed in this camp!

I know I have said enough, but I must tell you all I can about it. And I want you to let everybody read it. Americans are far too soft and realize too little, all that goes on. When I think of how German P.O.W.'s are treated and pampered by us in the states! It makes your blood boil!

Their housing conditions were worse than any slum could ever be. The double decker beds were pushed together and three slept to an average single bed. They could not be on their back – just on their side. No mattress – just a couple of blankets. And no air and one wash room for five hundred (500!) of them, where water was on one hour daily! And in that wash room, they had to wash the dishes, too! And 250 lived in each room and those rooms were no bigger than our ground floor at home. In the newer and brick buildings, there were two thousand to rooms only several times longer that the wooden barracks just mentioned. It was really unbelievably crowded. Of course, in the past week, ten thousand have been removed from the camp and conditions are now much less crowded. But, still it is.

For the ill – tuberculosis and such, they are stuck in one end of the camp called contagion. In stall-like, very shallow troughs and measuring about eight-foot square, they put over ten patients, six if they were post-operative - no mattress and only one blanket. And really – absolutely no toilet facilities!

The commander of the post lived close by with his wife and eight kids. In a bombing raid by our fliers in August, his wife and children were killed, but no P.O.W.'s. They made direct hits on the munition and iron works there, but did not hit one barracks. The P.O.W.'s are still marveling at the precision bombing. By the way, the commander has fled. His wife must have been a horrible person. For example, if a P.O.W. came in and there was a tattoo on his chest she liked, the tattoo was removed and prisoner killed. The tattoos were tanned and made into a purse or lamp shade! I did not see them, but others did, for they were on display until today. Isn't that hard to believe? It also seems she was quite fond of horses, so he ordered riding stables built for her by the P.O.W.'s to be completed by a certain date. On that date, it still was not quite completed, so three hundred workers were lined up and shot! Just a few examples of it.

In the laboratories, prisoners were used for experimentation – such as for which we use only guinea pigs and mice. Once, they went in, they never came out alive. They used to inject a dose of typhus into them, and then withdraw their blood and inject it into another prisoner!

In the operating room of three tables, they have an average of twenty minor cases daily. We met the three doctors – all prisoners from Czechoslovakia – averaging fifty years of age. Very pathetic to see. Kind faces and such sad eyes.

We saw about everything there. So, if you see anything in the papers about a German concentration camp and all the atrocities they name, just believe it, for incredible though it may seem, it is so – for I have seen enough to make me realize they will do anything. What they expect to gain is beyond me. I do not know. But Hell itself is too good for them.

I could go on, but today has been an ordeal and I am tired. I just wanted you to know of all this while I felt like writing about it.

Keep writing and send this to Julia. I can only write it all once.

Love to all,   Alice

"My mother saved this letter for me and I have shown it – along with photos we took at the time – to many people. Many people did not really believe that this had truly happened – until then. In my experience, the younger generation who were not born until much later, were more apt to accept it as factual. Yet I know very little if anything of this horror is taught in our schools. And this is so wrong. This must never happen again – anywhere – to any people. But what about Cambodia, Somalia, China and Bosnia? Is there not a degree of repetition? The Holocaust (meaning "total burning") must never be forgotten! The Nazis murdered over six million Jews and three million political dissidents and societal misfits – how could this ever be forgotten! I am so pleased that Holocaust Memorial museums are finally being built in this country. Every high school student – at least – should have to go through one.

After seeing the concentration camps, General Eisenhower said that until then, he had been told many soldiers did not really know what they were fighting for. He said camps would surely show them what they were fighting against.

There was no help for the sick prisoners. If they went out and worked and fell down and died, well, that was that. They were weak and they were starved. It was difficult to draw a comparison between the evac hospital's care of their prisoners and the Nazi care of their prisoners. The enlisted German P.O.W.'s were happy to being in the evac hospital. They said it was not their war. They didn't want war. It was the officers' war. The evac hospital's first reaction to having German P.O.W.'s was, "We have to put up with them." But then you realize, these are kids that should be home at school. They were so indoctrinated, they had no choice. The German officers knew they were doing the wrong thing.

It was just utter disbelief that anyone could hate another people so, to be so inhumane. And there were doctors, they were medical men and it's just, to us, doctors were good people who wanted to learn and foremost, wanted to help that individual. But these, they knew, they knew that death would result and there was no medical care for these sick people.

I didn't realize at the time, that what I witnessed, would never leave my mind. Some of our nurses came back to the evac and picked flowers and brought them in – maybe in memory of those who had died at the camp. It was such a contrast – sweet smelling flowers full of life and beauty. It was life affirming. It made me realize there is such a thing as 'man's inhumanity to man'. "

Buchenwald did not gas any prisoners. They did not have the facilities for that. They cremated prisoners that died in their camp and dead prisoners from other concentration camps.

Only five days after setting up in Nohra, the 45th Evac Hospital was instructed to set up inside Buchenwald Concentration Camp to treat several hundred patients. Some patients were evacuated to other hospitals. The doctors evaluated the prisoners and the enlisted men cared for them. A tremendous number of the patients had tuberculosis, typhus, diphtheria and lice. As the colonel had sent the nurses on leave, it put an extra burden on the enlisted men. Facilities had to be thoroughly cleaned to make them suitable for a hospital. The prisoners needed to be bathed, treated for lice and gradually fed high calorie solid food.

Alice and her unit tour Buchenwald Concentration Camp.
Alice is the short person without a helmet.

Ovens in crematorium

Ashes under gallows to be put in trenches

Massive trenches for human ash disposal

This poor man had to be carried out. Mentally affected he refused to leave!

Prisoner being carried out of bunk house that refused to leave

Funeral of an inmate - after

Funeral of prisoner after camp liberation

Three prisoners to a bunk so small, they had to sleep on their sides

The U.S. Army interrupted this cremation

Truckload of bodies awaiting cremation

This was another form of punishment

Prisoners picking up flyers dropped by Allied troops upon liberation

Liberation parade

FRENCH RIVIERA, FRANCE

May 4, 1945   French Riviera

Dearest Julia,

    If you have been quite observant and paid attention to all parts of a letter, you will no doubt be astounded and by rights and quite natural – envision – as to my present location. Yes dear, I am on a seven-day leave down in the French Riviera! We are in a small suburb called Juan-les-Pins, a few miles out of Cannes. "All this and Heaven, too", is what we keep on saying to ourselves. But let me try to start at the beginning. Day before yesterday, word came around, that any of us wanting to go down, were to sign up. Of course, I did, expecting to go, with luck, some day before we were all sent home. Then came the good word – you leave – all of you – twenty-five of us – in the morning at ten. What a job. A mad rush for the iron and wash basin! And finally comes the A.M. And the better news yet – we fly! One thousand miles, no less! And it is a four-day trip by regular G.I. means. So, at one o'clock, we catch a plane - C-47 – and take off - in midst of a hail, snow and sleet storm. Cold and windy – brrr! How welcome the south would be after that! (south of France, of course!) Well, it was just as windy up there and I think we found every air pocket there was in that thousand miles! It was the first air trip for quite a few and soon the cry was "Do you have any bucket here? I was feeling quite proud of myself, then, the first thing I knew, I was looking at the inside of a bucket myself! At one time, there were three trying to hit our bucket! Quite a spectacle it was! I did not feel very good during the whole trip and was really glad to hit old terra firma. But the scenery by air is simply beautiful. The first part is all fertile fields – plowed and sown and looking like so many patchwork quilts. And then dense forests and finally hills gradually getting higher

– the Alps with their snow-capped peaks, very few homes, really and finally the azure blue of the Mediterranean Sea. A very rocky coast and it was just as I have always pictured Rio de Janeiro – palm trees and sand and lovely Spanish homes and beautiful hotels. Oh, Julia, it is the most beautiful spot I have ever seen or hope to see! And all I wish, is that you were here to fully enjoy it with me. It took us nine hours almost to fly here – quite a long trip, but oh, how well worth it!

And our hotel! I shall enclose a folder for I could not start to describe it. Modern and beautiful and comfort! Oh, la, la! Vicky and I have a lovely large room – two big and wonderful beds, a private bath with all the hot water you want and a private balcony – every room has one! And we look out and see the sea. And the dining room is facing the sea and the food, although regular army food, is prepared so well and served so nicely, you would hardly recognize it.

It is a little cool to go bathing yet, but we can walk, shop, bike, go on tours and do and wear anything we please! Of course, all we own are uniforms, but we don't wear ties and are just comfortable. And today, Vicky and I got a lovely permanent each and then had our hair set a la Francois! Quite the stuff, but you know how it will be in the A.M.

You can get any man you want here – they are beaucoup! But we stayed in tonight to write a few letters and rest. Tomorrow, we shop in Antibes and go to Cannes and I do not know what else! I'll try to find you something pretty if you are good.

Gee, I wish you were here. It reminds me so of our trip to Wildwood! I wrote Mother already, so now I must sign off. Keep writing and be good.

All my love and I truly miss you now more than ever,   Al

Alice and Vicky arrive in the Riviera

May 5, 1945   French Riviera

Dearest Mother and All,

Just a start to a little letter as I wait for Vicky to return from mass. I would like to go to church today, but you have to go all the way to Cannes and I hate to go alone.

Today is another very lovely day. Clear and sunny and as I looked out from my balcony, I see they are going to serve our breakfast outdoors on the terrace. The terrace is black and white tile and the tables and chairs are red. All around are flowers, especially roses of all colors and shrubbery lines the wall. It is really very grand. Attractive French girls in black and white and our excellent head waiter. So, you see it is really very much the same as if we were Mrs. Vanderbilt and following!

This morning after breakfast, Vicky and I are going hiking. We have not yet picked out our route. Yesterday afternoon, we took a two-hour bike ride all up and down the coast line and how very beautiful it is. Earlier in the day, we went into Cannes as our planned over a two-hour cruise along the coast. But the sea was too rough and they cancelled the trip. So, we go on that on Tuesday.

Several hours later

Well, we had our bike ride and what a grand day it is! For miles we biked into Antibes and all along the coastal road. In the distance, you can see the mountains through a haze and the sea is a real azure blue. The homes are so beautiful, too. Everyone is a colorful and picturesque as can be. We biked for hours and that is the best way to see their country. This afternoon, we plan on going for a ride in little boats they call pedals, for you pedal them while they are in the water to make them ride. It looks like a lot of fun and I shall be able to tell you more of it later.

And of course, to make everything perfect, it looks as if this war will really be over before we finish our leave here. Maybe it is already over. I have not heard the latest news. But last night, they had the big, coastal guns in Cannes all ready to fire to celebrate and announce the end. I cannot believe it. It just does not seem possible that it really is almost over after all of these years. I have said I do not want to go home until the whole war was over, but now I know I want to go home as soon as I can. That is certain. This little touch of real freedom has made me realize how very much I want to go home. I want to try to make up for all the time I have lost. I want to see and be with each one of you. It has been so long since we were all together. So, come the first opportunity, I shall take a boat to the U.S.A.! The very thought of it gives me chills of pleasure and excitement. I am thrilled even when I think of it.

I must go down to dinner, so I'll continue later.

8:30 P.M.

Here I sit and am I sun-burned! You burn so much quicker and easier here than even at the shore for some reason. I found that out today! First Vicky and I got a 'pedal' and had an hour's worth of fun and sun. You recline in a canvas chair and pedal this pontoon-like boat. And really, they are the cutest thing. Then, we laid on the beach for over an hour and really, both of us got a good start on a real tan. Tomorrow, we are again going to hike and sunbathe after dinner to keep our tan going good.

Perhaps you wonder why I never mention the evenings or nights here. Well, all they do is dance and drink and it is too hard to try to meet someone who does not. So, we take a short walk in the evening and then come in to write, read or sleep.

But it is a perfect place and a wonderful vacation. I love it here and only wish you could be along to enjoy it - all of you.

Keep writing and I'll perhaps see you someday not too far away.

Love to all,   Alice

May 8, 1945 V. E. Day   French Riviera
Dearest Mother and All,

Today is the day we have all waited for so long. It just does not seem possible that it is now here. I still cannot realize that there shall be no more fighting and killing over here. Thank God there shall not be! If only there was no more in the Pacific. May it soon be over there, too. And then we shall have real reason to thank God. Until that day does arrive, it really shall not seem as if this war is over.

For several days we have been waiting for the good news. The guns have been ready to fire forth their military salute for three days and today, at three o'clock, after Churchill's speech, they really let loose! In fact, it sounded more like our first days in Normandy than a declaration of peace! And ever since, all day, including the present hour, they are still firing at different points along the coast.

At three, we had just come in from a long bike ride, in time to hear the conclusion of Churchill's speech and "God bless the King." Then the guns started, so we went out, down to the beach and watched them fire the guns. It was then, that it really dawned on us that the war was over and Germany was defeated! And it was there you just stopped and breathed a prayer of thanks to God for all of His blessings and care during this awful siege. And the rest of the day, you kept on saying to yourself and to those around you – "Is it really a fact at last?" or "It just does not seem possible, does it?" We still do not fully grasp the meaning of it. But all over town are papers in the shop windows "Finis la guerre!" If only we could now go directly home, instead of waiting around over here. And now we begin to wonder what they will do with us, for there is no use for an evac hospital now. I only hope they do not break our unit up. I would hate that.

Tonight, Vicky and I went into a little French Catholic chapel that is next to the hotel – a beautiful place. There was a service going on and it was just the right place, somehow, to give thanks to God for all He has done for us. There is such a spirit of reverence in the Catholic chapels. Anyway, it was good to be there.

There is so much I want to say today, but you must realize all there could be said - we are all thinking and praying for one thing – a soon return to home!

Good night dear and may God keep each of you and bring us all together soon.

Love always,   Alice

May 8, 1945 V. E. Day   French Riviera

Dearest Julia,

At last, it is here - the day we have longed for and I just can't believe it is here. That all fighting is over on this side of the world and that Germany is no longer is our enemy – but our prisoner! As the day goes on, it is now eleven at night – I realize more fully that it is V-Day over here. I just wrote Mother and now writing to you, I realize all the more how much it means, for it brings it closer and clearer to me. It means that now it just cannot be too long until we are returned to our homes. Somehow, I now feel that they will not send us to the C.B.I. It just seems as if they could not do that to us now – for some reason. And I do not want to go. All I want now is to go home. I realize that clearly now. I know it will still be a matter of months before we can be sent home, but at least this is the beginning of the end for us. If only the war in the Pacific were over, too! May it please God to see a soon end to that, too.

Julia, I am so homesick tonight! It is the night I want particularly to be with all of you. We all should be together to thank God for His mercies and goodness. Vicky and I did go into a little French chapel that is next to our hotel, and it was lovely. Such an air of peace and reverence, and they were having a service of their own. But it was somehow, the proper place to give God the praise and glory we ought to and it was just good to be there – even if their service did not mean a thing to us being in French – to me anyway.

All day long, the guns here have been firing and it sounds like a war is starting! They have been ready to fire for three days now and so they are really doing a good job of it now!

This morning when we read the headlines of The Stars and Stripes – "Unconditional Surrender Announced by Germany". The chills just ran up and down me! And to hear Churchill speak on the radio – and that just made it final – I had a hard time to keep from crying for joy.

I can think of only one better place to celebrate V. E. Day – home. But the Riviera is a beautiful place. Every day, the more I see of it, the more I realize it. It is simply unbelievable to think of so much beauty in one spot. Someday, I will try to describe it to you.

I have so much I want to say and ought to say in this letter, but I know you are feeling all I feel, so you perhaps understand.

Good night and may God keep you

Love always,   *Al*

"Can it really be here? The day we have prayed for and hoped for, for so long? Yes, the war was finally over – this was that long-awaited day. After all those long, awful months we would have peace! We did realize that this would not mean we would return to the United States soon- but we did know that we would be going. Certainly, there would be no reason to send us to the C.B.I. now. The fighting here now was over – no more killing or wounded and no more bombs or guns or tanks or planes. This was Peace!

All that now remains will be the same good news from the Pacific front. We realized that this war was not really over until Japan surrendered. How could they continue?

This was the perfect ending to a very perfect leave. We could now only wait for good news from Japan.

Now that the war in our theater was over, our concern was that we would experience a period when our spirits would drop as we all knew that when we returned, there was a great probability that our outfit would gradually be scattered. This was what would be happening throughout the army, and that would be very difficult to accept. We were so like a large family! But the Army was working on a "point system" which would decide which individuals would be sent back to the States. This system had yet to be perfected."

NOHRA, GERMANY

May 13, 1945 Mothers' Day   Germany

Dearest Mother,

Just a few lines to let you know I am thinking of you today in a very extra special way, for today is truly your day, in every sense of the words "Mothers' Day". And what a wonderful mother you have always been to us, and still are! If only words could fully express all I would like to write to you tonight. To try to tell you how much you mean to me – so much more ever since I have been overseas and so utterly away from you. To know I could always sit down and write you and you would fully understand no matter how I would write and more important than anything else, to know you were faithfully praying for me every day and I know that has helped me always. But most important of all, you have taught us about our Savior from early childhood. It is through you, that today, we have the full knowledge of Christ as our own Savior. And how all important that is, for although we may not always live the way a Christian ought, we still know He loves us and will never forsake us.

Today, Sunday, we had a special Mothers' Day service at the main chapel. An outside chaplain spoke and gave an excellent sermon. He picked an odd text for his talk – Luke 2:35. "Yea, a sword shall pierce through thy own soul, also" – Simeon speaking to Mary after blessing Christ. He spoke of Mary as mother of Christ, and all she went through as a mother. He brought it all out beautifully. Mothers' Day always means so much to us over here, for we realize what a mother really means and how we have missed our own mothers.

I am enclosing a little poem written by a soldier – he seems to have expressed it pretty well.

I will close – saying and meaning it with all I have – Thank God for giving me a mother like you – the best and dearest mother any girl, or fellow, could ever wish for or hope to have. May God bless you always and keep you safe.

All my love always,   Alice

"The 45th Evacuation Hospital was awarded the 'Award of Meritorious Service Unit Plaque' in honor and recognition for our 'superior performance of duty in accomplishment of exceptionally difficult tasks during December 2, 1944 through February 16, 1945, during the Battle of the Bulge during the Ruhr Offensive.'

It was very gratifying to be recognized for superior performance in a difficult time. The outward manifestation of this honor was a special patch we attached to the lower sleeve of our uniform."

SANKT WENDEL, GERMANY

June 16, 1945   Germany, Anniversary of D-10

Dearest Mother and All,

Exactly one year ago today, this same time of the day, we had our D-Day. What a day that was! We left Southampton the night before, but our ship stayed in harbor close by until daylight. Then we set forth. You can well imagine what a busy place the channel was, for that was only the tenth day after D-Day. Ships and planes of every description! Guns and shells could be heard as we approached. Then, after we got fairly close, we all got aboard L82's and went ashore. It is a feeling I shall never forget – now could I ever fully describe it. A feeling, headed by the inevitable question – what next? They had built, already, a landing dock of sorts and we were fortunate in not having to wade ashore. At least we stayed dry! What a sight that beach was! Ships wrecked all along the shore. All kinds of vehicles and equipment completely ruined and the hillside black from shelling and fire. We had to stay right on the beach for several hours until all of our immediate personnel arrived. In the not too great distance, we could hear the noises of battle – a noise we were to very soon get used to. And still, it did not seem as if it could be real. It was just something we expected and had planned to do, but never really thought the day would actually arrive. Finally, a truck came for us to take us to a field several miles away where we were to set our hospital up. We arrived in a shell and bomb marked field – one full of foxholes and deep pits the Germans had used – both for gun placements and trenches. Naturally, we were exhausted and hungry. So, we fixed us a "personal" fox hole and got it ready for the night. All the belongings we had with us was our musette bag with our personal belongings – and carried only a few things in it, as you would a small overnight bag. And a K-ration. We got supper and got ready to spend the night out. Then, word comes by our Executive Officer that our equipment and the rest of our personnel could not be unloaded from the ships as the channel was too rough, but we were to go over to an evac hospital that had arrived the day before and work there, for they were very busy. So out we get. Pack up our few articles and leave our fox holes. Really, we were glad to have something to do for just lying there knowing the planes would be over and snipers could be heard all around. And so, our experience in battle started. I went right on duty in surgery and worked all night. The cases were horrible – all the more, they seemed to us since they were the first battle casualties I had ever seen. Even after all I have seen since, I can still vividly recall those I saw that night and that week, for we stayed there for a week until our hospital was unloaded and set up close by. It was so good to get to work in our own hospital. Comparative to going home for us. But we were busy. We would come on duty and there would be anywhere from one hundred and fifty to three hundred cases to be done and we could only run eight to twelve tables at a time. We never caught up, for as fast as we sent these from surgery, they were replaced by a new arrival. I can look back on those days now and really wonder how we ever did all we did. It would not be too hard now, for we know what to expect and how to go about it. But it was all so new to us and yet it all ran so smoothly taking everything into consideration.

So, a year has passed and I hope we shall soon be seeing each other on American soil. I feel we shall. No matter what comes after, I shall be happy and satisfied to be with all of you for a few weeks. After the war - well that can't be _too_ long!

Write soon. Our mail is held up someplace for some reason. It is a long time since I heard.

Love always to all,   Alice

June 23, 1945   Germany

Dearest Mother and All,

I am afraid I have really neglected writing you this past week, but I was not in the mood – being on night duty for one reason and having nothing to write, for a second reason. No excuses for it – I know I ought to write anyway. But our mail is not coming in – has not for over three weeks. One day I got four letters and that is all. It is rather disheartening to say the least.

I guess you are anxious to know where we stand. So am I! We were told officially for a change, that we are going to C.B.I., but so far, we have not been told whether or not we go by way of the States. We have heard nothing at all about the possibility of our not going home, so we are quite optimistic. If so, it will undoubtedly be in the early fall. That is my assumption from all I have heard and can conclude. It is awful to know so little about so important a thing! If by any chance they send the outfit straight to the C.B.I., I am afraid they shall not be worth very much. They all need a trip home first.

We are really having beautiful summer weather now - warm and sunny. I am afraid I do not fully appreciate them. There is no place to go even if you wanted to.

Julia seems a lot happier now that she is more used to it. It does take quite a while to get used to a new camp. That is why I hate to get used to a new outfit.

I got the snaps of Johnny and Ruthie and they are darling. How I hope you and I can go down to see them. It ought to be a nice trip.

Perhaps one of these days I shall get a lot of mail. I need it badly. It always keeps up your morale.

Take care of yourself and do keep writing – all of you.

Love always,   Alice

"Once again, the probability of being sent to the C.B.I. seemed very real. Japan had not surrendered. And soon, we were officially told that this was the plan for us. We tried to accept this – but to us it seemed unfair. But you do learn in the service you just accept those orders. Now our concern was whether or not we could go directly to the C.B.I. – or go first to the States. We tried to be optimistic, but we needed that trip to the U.S. and we felt we had indeed earned it. Another concern was whether or not our hospital would be disbanded at a time when we so needed to be together.

We went through a series of moves – once again living in tents, and not feeling very needed. It really seemed so futile – long trips between each set up. No patients, so no hospital was needed. Our morale was at a very low point. We ended this series of moves in a little town in Bavaria. And it was here we learned we were in the Occupation Army, and scheduled for the C.B.I. by way of the U.S.! Now everything seemed in limbo. But we now had some direction – even if we were not happy about it."

SCHWABISCH HALL, GERMANY

July 14, 1945   Germany

Dearest Julia,

Well, here we are – out roughing it again after over seven months of buildings – even if those buildings did range from palatial hotels to stables! But last evening, we made a move into tents again. And it took a few hours to feel like "home" again, I assure you. Let me start from yesterday morning at the wee hour of four A.M. That is when we got up out of our deep sleep to get ready to depart by six. And at six, we left – in a G.I. truck – open – ready to begin our trip of almost two hundred miles. We were leaving the Fifteenth Army and going temporarily into the Seventh Army – supposedly to take over a hospital. And so, our trip started on a day that really promised to be hot and sunny. And it was. And dirty – we had to take quite a few dusty back roads and over fields on detours and the dust was so thick, it formed a cloud. And riding in the very back of a G.I. truck, I naturally got it. Never mind how I have been so tired and dirty and burned as I was when we arrived at our field at four P.M. The sun and wind burned our faces and eyes until it was terribly painful. To say nothing of our appearances! We finally got most of the grime off with a panful of cold water. Our trip took us from St. Wendel, Mannheim, Heidelberg and here to Schwab Hall, close to Bavaria – not too far from Stuttgart. Perhaps that gives you an idea of our location. The scenery of the trip was beautiful and we followed the Neckar River for quite some distance and that really made a beautiful ride, all along the river, with mountains on all sides and dense forests. We stopped along the way for a lunch of canned rations – really not too bad – baked beans and crackers plus some fruit juice and fresh lettuce and carrots we picked at our last area. And it broke up the long trip too.

When we finally got here, the payoff was that no one expected us and in fact, they thought we were the Army of Occupation and were quite surprised when we told them we were category #2 – (for C.B.I. via the States). So here we are – for no good reason and how long, we do not know. We are just taking it easy and enjoying life. If only some mail would come! Please write soon at my new APO of 758.

Nothing else new – just waiting and hoping to be home by October.

Love always,   Al

July 14, 1945   Germany

Dearest Mother and All,

Well, today was our moving day and I just want to drop you a note before crawling into bed. Here we are – out roughing it again after over seven months of buildings – even if those buildings did range from palatial hotels to stables! But last evening, we made a move into tents again. We were leaving the Fifteenth Army and going temporarily into the Seventh Army – supposedly to take over a hospital. And it took a few hours to feel like "home" again, I assure you. It was a trip of almost two hundred miles and a scorcher of a day. We got up at three-thirty this morning and left at six. Our trip took us from St. Wendel, Mannheim, Heidelberg and here to Schwab Hall, close to Bavaria – not too far from Stuttgart. Perhaps that gives you an idea of our location. The scenery of the trip was beautiful and we followed the Neckar River for quite some distance and that really made a beautiful ride, all along the river, with mountains on all sides and dense forests. We stopped along the way for a lunch of canned rations – really not too bad – baked beans and crackers plus some fruit juice and fresh lettuce and carrots we picked at our last area. We finally arrived at four this afternoon. Never have you seen such dirty, tired and wind-burned group of people! We rode in an open G.I. truck and the sun and wind have surely done us dirty! When we got to Hall, we were a far cry from American womanhood, you may be sure. Bridges were out and we had to make detours through dust fields. Towns were bombed out and dirt and rubble always found its way to us, especially our faces. Between dirt and burn, they are plenty sore and red now. And to top it all off, we are in the field living in tents again! It was a let-down, but I think I will like it again – after we get used to it. You ought to see our colonel's tent! All along, he has been gathering up all sorts and descriptions of furniture – over-stuffed chairs, an inner-spring mattress – complete with bed and bureau. And he has all that stuff in his tent! So, you may be sure if he can find any place in a house to live, he will not stay in a tent!

It seems we are done here, so we shall be in American occupied territory and shall not set up or work. Just rest! Again!

Our fellows in the Mess did a wonderful job of our Mess tent and supper tonight. After that long trip and heat, they set up the tent – complete with tables, chairs, table cloths and gave us steak! It was a wonderful meal and all done so nicely. I do not know how they did it. It was all we could do to set up our beds and take a spit bath!

And so, now to bed. Our new APO is 758 – so please use it in the future. That is Seventh Army - we are now attached to them.

Nothing else new – just waiting and hoping to be home by October.

I'll write a letter tomorrow. This is just a note.

Love to all always,   Alice

BRETTEN, GERMANY

July 24, 1945   Germany

Dearest Mother and All,

Another move to add to our already long list of moves since we have hit Europe. This time, it was a trip of only sixty miles and not too bad.

July 27, 1945   Germany

And that is as far as I got in my good intentions of writing! We are not at all busy – just work every other day and they're not even a full day! But just the fact that we are set up and acting as a station hospital, does make the time pass more quickly. The week we were in the field passed so slowly. Now time is going more like we want it.

We are set up in a school building. Our wing of it was bombed out, so you can perhaps picture it. Very few panes of glass and boards where glass ought to be. So, if you open the windows to get some fresh air and daylight, you have flies as an extra gift. The flies here are terrible and no wonder at all! The Germans are not normally too strict as far as sanitation goes and with conditions as they are now, the flies are awful. Undoubtedly, there are plenty of bodies under all the bombed homes and buildings, and the flies are in abundance. We are in the process of getting screens made. By the time we get them made, it will be time to leave here.

Our quarters are in a private home and Vicky and I are quite fortunate in having a nice room together. Our mess hall is on the first floor of the house and we have German girls as waitresses. Our food was awful for the first few days, but is improving regularly. Even to ice cream – and it is so good on these hot days. Cool in the morning and at night, but the middle of the day is a scorcher. The lady who owns our house was the wife of the former burgermeister, or mayor, and when the Americans took over the town, he fed her and all the family poison and then committed suicide. Fortunately, he did not give her and one daughter enough poison, so they are still alive. Two other daughters died along with their father. Every home would present quite a tragic tale, I am sure. And all for the cause of a few! How much Hitler and his followers have to answer for!

Finally, so mail is coming in and how wonderful it is to hear from you all again. So far, I have heard once each from you, Fran, Julia and Eileen. Recent letters, too.

I still plan on being home sometime this fall. I cannot see how they can keep us over any longer. But, of course, the Army can do as they please! How well I know that! I cannot figure out how Pauline is home already, unless they are going to the C.B.I. We really have been tossed all around since First Army left. No one seems to realize we are still over here. As long as they do not forget us or the time we are supposed to leave.

We have heard the various rumored reports about Japan and the proposals of surrender and her terms. If it would mean an end of all this slaughter of our men, I am for it. But I can't see how it would work if we did not occupy Japan. They should be made to accept our terms.

Well, I'll mail this now and write soon. I must write Julia now. All is well here and I am trusting all is so at home. Give my love to all – you know who I include in that.

Love to all of you always,   Alice

Main Street - Bombed -out stores and homes

Bretten, Germany – main street bombed out

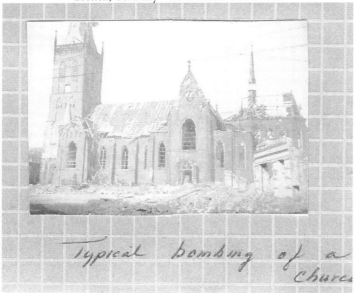

Typical bombing of a Church

Bombed church in Germany

August 18, 1945   Germany

Dearest Mother and All,

Praise God the war is finally over! It does not seem at all possible that this can be so - that in no place is there any more killing

177

and destruction. It's going to take a little while to really fully compre-hend this wonderful thing called peace. It must have been one happy and thankful day for you folks at home – more so really than for us over here, for our day was the day Germany capitulated. But it is all so very wonderful – how very many homes this is a Godsend to. I am thinking in particular of Annie – how thankful she must be and how fortunate Frankie is. We have been waiting around here for days – in anticipation of the Japanese surrender and finally last night when there was no further news at midnight, I went to bed. And at one A.M. the noise really let loose, for it was then that the radio announced the wonderful words of peace. Such celebrating! But it is so grand for so many of the fellows over here were quite prepared to go to the Pacific – of no choice of their own. And now, of course, that is out. You can imagine how they must feel!

I'll try to get in a trip to the Bavarian Alps next week. It is a four-day trip by truck and it comes eight hundred miles, but it is supposed to be well worth all of the discomfort you may suffer. It includes the hideout of Hitler, Brennan Pass and all of that country. And those who have come from such trips, say the scenery is unusu-ally beautiful, deep in the Alps, so you can imagine. If I do go, I prom-ise a full and detailed report on it.

I know you feel better now you realize Johnny will not return to the Pacific. How truly wonderful that is!

Take care of yourself and keep writing.

Love always to all,   Alice

August 15, 1945   Germany

Dearest Julia,

Well, are you folks back home still celebrating Victory Day? From all accounts, the celebrations were really quite the thing. I must say that our Victory celebrations were all on the quiet and subdued side. Naturally, there were, and in fact, still are, those individuals who went in for celebration in a big way! The one thing that really impressed me, was an event that took place just after the news came through at one in the morning. One of our officers slightly under the influence of, took out his bugle and player the Star-Spangled Banner. It sounded really beautiful and certainly gave us all a very great thrill. You know how just hearing it at home makes you feel. Well, then imagine how you would feel hearing it under those circumstances – especially when you do not hear it once a year even. It was beautiful.

Now quite naturally, all of our interest is in getting home and as soon as possible. And everything looks like it is in our favor. Points being lowered and all of the planes and ships concentrated on taking troops home. What a morale booster this is! And what a great difference you can notice in all of the men. It does you good to see it.

I'm planning on going to Berchtesgaden on Wednesday for a four-day trip through the Bavarian Alps. It is supposed to be a beautiful trip and also quite an interesting one. It is long and tiring, being over eight hundred miles by truck – and that is not easy riding! But those who have already come back say it is well worth the trip. So, I am looking forward to going and it ought to make an interesting letter, too – or perhaps I can tell you about it.

Love,   Alice

SALZBURG, AUSTRIA, OBERAMMERGAU, GERMANY AND BERCHTESGADEN, BAVARIA

"At a time when we so needed some pleasant diversion, we were given passes and transportation to see more of this spectacular country – Bavaria and Germany. Granted, our transportation was our old faithful truck, but we were used to this and we were happy to have such an opportunity to have such a pleasant diversion.

Our major trip was to the Bavarian Alps and down to Berchtesgaden. There were to be several wonderful side trips. This was a round trip of over 700 miles, covering so many places of interest and great beauty. Bavaria was one of the most beautiful areas I have ever seen. In fact, the beauty of Germany as a whole was unsurpassed. We drove through many miles of dense forests and craggy mountain ranges – little towns with story book homes – all colorfully painted with pictures of both religious and nature scenes. It must sound very peculiar, but they were masterpieces of great talent and beauty. Most of the buildings had window boxes filled with cascading flowers and vines at the upper window level.

Everything was fresh and colorful and spotless. There was no evidence of war and destruction any place. Actually, the city of Munich, Germany was the only area we passed through that showed evidence of war – and the city was virtually destroyed.

I would never forget Salzburg, an old, historical and beautiful city. It was very mountainous with the river flowing through the center. On the top of several very high hills, were ancient castles – really fortresses. We took a cable car to the most famous one, and had a tour of it. It was indeed out of this world – and centuries into the past. We went down into its depths and saw the torture chambers and dungeon – with all the primitive tools of torture. We were glad to leave that section and go outside to another level. We stood on the old ramparts and looked out over the lovely city of Salzburg. This was indeed breathtaking.

On to Oberammergau – the home of the famous Passion Play. The village was snuggled in the peaceful valley on a large lake surrounded by the mountains. We saw several of the actors who lived in the area. In appearance, they certainly lived like the man who walked with Christ in the early day of the apostles.

Berchtesgaden was our final destination on this trip. It was here that Hitler had his infamous mountain-top retreat – the Eagle's Nest. This was accessible only by an elevator system – built into the mountain. It was truly an architectural wonder, for under the mountain was a great network of facilities – restaurant, guest house, barracks, medical and dental offices, and other ancillary offices.

On the very top of the mountain was the Eagle's Nest where Hitler had his Bavarian headquarters and home. Several of the ranking officers of his "cabinet" had big homes in the vicinity. We were able to see the bombed-out ruins of the homes of Goering and Borman, and were allowed to walk through the rubble. They did live in luxury.

The small town of Berchtesgaden was in an ideal location – such a peaceful setting now. We were in a fine, modern hotel – yet it maintained the atmosphere of old Bavaria. It was so comfortable – and it was here that we were introduced to fine feather beds and down comforters – light as a cloud – and so warm and cozy in the cold mountain air.

It was a wonderful trip and did so much to give all of us that needed lift for our spirits which had hit a low. The return trip was through country that was not equaled by any other part of the world that we had seen.

Shortly after we returned from Bavaria, we heard that wonderful news – Japan surrendered!

That day had finally come, this terrible war was over, and now we knew we would not go to the C.B.I.! We would soon be on our way home to the U.S.A. Of course, the most important thing was there would be no more fighting and death and destruction. Now we would just wait for orders and hope they would be for our return.

We were in Bretten, Germany, near Stuttgart in September when we finally received those orders – to report to Marseilles, France, where we would wait for further orders for sailing home! We were now on the point system – a complicated system – and only one other nurse and I had sufficient points to qualify for return to the States. We had such mixed emotions – we were going home – but we were leaving behind such wonderful friends and co-workers. We knew this was really good-bye, and that did hurt."

Elevator to "Eagle's Nest"

Hitler's bombed out home "Eagle's Nest"

MARSEILLES, FRANCE

September 6, 1945   France

Dearest Julia,

Now we have gotten as far as Marseilles on our trip to the States – and from here, I do not know the score. Today, we are supposed to find out what our date of sailing is to be, so I'll hold off the mailing of this letter until then. We got down here on Monday morning and our hopes were so high – we fully expected to leave here within a couple of days, but we still sit. It is a project that has been mismanaged from the start. They have been sending out nurses from here all along with only thirty points! And finally, they wised up and started bringing down all the nurses with ninety or more points to the Staging Area here. We are to replace the nurses who are now truly sweating out a sailing date! Four of us came down from the outfit together.

We first learned about our orders last Friday night after we got back from seeing a musical comedy in Heidelberg – we were excited, for we were first told we were to fly and that meant we would come home on Tuesday. Then our orders came in and we were informed we were to fly to Paris and from there to Marseille to join the Seventh Convalescent Hospital. So, after a lot of trouble in trying to get on the flight to Paris, we arrive in Marseilles – only to find that the Seventh was the Staging Area and not an outfit sailing for home! That was indeed a terrible let down! And no one down here seemed to know what the score was. We were assigned quarters and from then on, no one told us a thing! We finally did have a meeting yesterday and after we learn our sailing date, we just wait – some more. But it is not too bad here. Quarters are good – at least we are not in tents as so many staging areas are – and all E.M. and officers are, too. The food is excellent – and you can buy all the ice cream you wish and cokes. There are plenty of movies here and in Marseille, but the city is an awful place. Dirty and crowded and nothing there of any interest. We went yesterday and were glad to come back. It is just this awful waiting that is hard to take. And it was hard to leave the unit, too. For I had several good friends there – and naturally, Vicky did not have enough points to come along. I hated to say goodbye to her. I also hated to say goodbye to the sergeant I told you about from surgery. I know I wrote and told you that I had changed my feelings toward him, but I am afraid I was only fooling myself – for I had a date with him the night before I left and it was wonderful! It is a thing of the past, I know, but I certainly cherish the memories. That is what I hate about this Army – make friends and then leave. Perhaps I can someday explain myself easier to you in words – and soon!

Julia, we are all nervous wrecks waiting to be assigned! You can perhaps understand, to a certain degree, how we must feel! Two years away from everyone that means everything to us – and now the chance comes for us to go home! Maybe I'll be home before you get this letter! I'll call you as soon as I can so you can arrange for a leave – I still can't believe we'll all be together again! I'll hold off finishing this letter until after our meeting that takes place in an hour for I ought to be able to tell you something definite by then! Am I excited? I surely am! I can't concentrate on this letter any longer – be back with you in a little while, dear!

Later

Well, here I am again and the news I bring is too, too wonder-ful! We ought to load the ship tomorrow! We are sailing as part of the 250th General – and are scheduled to sail Saturday or Sunday! Julia, I can't yet believe it! It all seems like a dream that I shall awaken from!

So, be on your toes and be ready to ask for that long awaited leave!

I'm on my way home, Julia, I am finally on my way home!

185

Hold tight and I'll soon see you.

Love always,   *Al*

"Finally, our orders came through and we were on the U.S.S. Breckenridge on our way home! We sailed through the spectacular Straits of Gibraltar and on out into the Atlantic Ocean. This was a very different trip than the one we had made almost two years ago. In less than a week, we were in the United States — not in New York harbor, and so we missed seeing the Statue of Liberty — but somehow, that was not important. We were home!"

EPILOGUE

The 45th Evacuation Hospital moved their station at least 20 times, breaking down camp, packing camp, unpacking camp, cleaning and sterilizing equipment. At the beginning of their European tour, they had 40+ officers, 40+ nurses, over 200 enlisted men, 20+ vehicles and 20+ trailers. When set up, they had 400 beds and treated over 10,000 patients.

"The 45th Evacuation Hospital was awarded the Meritorious Service Unit Plaque in recognition for their "superior performance of duty in accomplishment of exceptionally difficult tasks during December 2, 1944, through February 16, 1945 during the Battle of the Bulge during the Ruhr Offensive." It was very gratifying to be recognized for superior performance in a difficult time."

Alice continued to work as a nursing supervisor for forty more years in various states. Her sister, Julia's move to Detroit drew Alice to Michigan and a position at Blodgett Hospital in Grand Rapids as a nursing supervisor. Alice's sister, Julia, married her Scottish doctor. Alice never married and died in 2005.

"After a wonderful reunion with family and friends – and well-deserved thirty-day leave – I was assigned to Fort Meade, Maryland. I found little challenge in the peace time Army – it was not what I had anticipated, so I applied for an honorable discharge – which I was granted on May 19, 1946, from Fort Dix, New Jersey, with rank of Captain. I had entered the Army in early June, 1941, exactly five years before. I will always look back on those five years in the Army as some of the best years of my nursing career of forty-five years! They fulfilled a dream and goal I had and certainly shaped my further pursuits in nursing. Putting my experiences on paper – reliving those years – has been a remarkable and satisfying experience for me – in my retirement years."

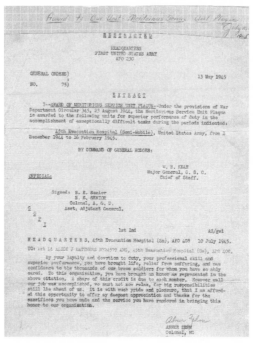

Meritorious Service Unit Plaque for the 45th Evacuation Hospital

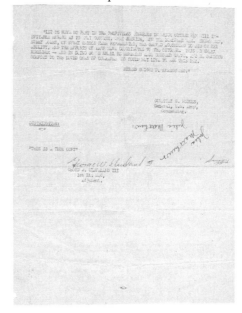

Alice's mother Matilda, at her front door. Notice the stars in the side window. Families would put stars on the front of their houses to show that they had a family member in the service. Matilda's door had three stars – Alice, Julia and Johnny.

Alice's Stations Through Her Military Career

May 1941	Camp Forrest, Tennessee
Summer 1943	Camp Gordon, Georgia
November 7, 1943	Fort Dix, New Jersey
November 17, 1943	Aboard the Aquitania
November 24, 1943	Firth of Clyde, Scotland
November 25, 1943	Wotten-Under-Edge, England
June 15, 1944	Southampton, England
June 16, 1944	Omaha Beach, Normandy (D+10)
June 16, 1944	La Cambe, France
July 25, 1944	Airel, France
August 9, 1944	Saint-Sever, France
August 22, 1944	Senoches, France
September 5, 1944	La Capelle, France
September 16, 1944	Baelen, Belgium
September 28, 1944	Eupen, Belgium
December 31, 1944	Jodoigne, Belgium
January 19, 1945	Spa, Belgium
March 5, 1945	Eschweiler, Germany
March 25, 1945	Honnef, Germany
April 3, 1945	Bad Wildungen, Germany
April 22, 1945	Nohra, Germany
April 28, 1945	Buchenwald Concentration Camp, Germany
May 11, 1945	Nohra, Germany
June 4, 1945	Sankt Wendel, Germany (operating as a station hospital under the Fifteenth U.S. Army)
July 14, 1945	Schwabisch Hall, Germany (bivouac with the Seventh U.S. Army)
July 22, 1945	Bretten, Germany (operating as a station hospital under the 106th Infantry Division)
September 23, 1945	Marseilles, France – to depart Europe on the USS Brechenridge

A NOTE FROM THE AUTHOR

Alice always had a very good feeling towards the Jewish people. Her mother had embedded that feeling in her as a child. They felt that the Jews were God's chosen people and they believed in God. Her military experience strengthened her faith and made her feel she must always speak out about the Holocaust and defend the Jewish people. She shared her experiences and her memories of what she had seen at Buchenwald with her family and friends, newspapers, her church and the Holocaust Memorial Center in West Bloomfield, Michigan. She wanted everyone to know that the Holocaust was real. It did happen. And it must never happen again!

I remember visits by my Aunt Alice to our home, in the same house that Alice grew up in, on Monument Avenue. In our home, Alice was always a revered hero. I remember being told as a child, "You better be good when your aunt comes. She was in the Army you know!"

Just a few years ago, I was given a copy of my Aunt Alice's memoir, "Lest We Forget" that she wrote in 1993 from her letters home. With my father Eddie's passing in 2019, a box was found in the back of his closet, filled with 81 letters Aunt Alice had written home. These were just a small number of all the letters she had written home from her service in Europe. I found it fascinating to read about how this young girl of twenty-two courageously left all she knew to serve our country. Alice's story has made me laugh at moments and at other times, cry for her. Then I watched a video interview of Aunt Alice by Donna Sklar of The Zekelman Holocaust Center, Farmington Hills, Michigan, which was conducted in 1995. I felt very strongly that Alice's story must be told to more than just her family and close friends. She had a mission of letting everyone know about the truth and reality of German concentration camps. She felt there was no 'inferior' race and there was no 'superior' race. We are who our character is, we are not our skin color. We are defined by our treatment of each other.

ABOUT THE AUTHOR

Mary Matthews Fetterman grew up in Malvern, Pennsylvania, down the street from the Paoli Memorial Grounds. She has been exploring her family's history for the past decade. Several members of Mary's family have served in the military, including her brother David, who served in the Navy during the Vietnam war. She shows her appreciation for the sacrifices made to preserve our freedoms by regularly placing flags on service members' graves and anonymously sending flags to neighbors flying tattered flags.

Mary is a proud mother of two sons, Andrew and Kevin and grandmother to granddaughter, Lulu. She is an avid gardener and stained glass artist. Mary lives in Lancaster County, Pennsylvania with her husband, Jim and their dog Max.

Mary wanted to carry out her Aunt Alice's greatest wish – to ensure that we don't forget about the sacrifices that were made by our service men and women and to tell everyone the truth of the Holocaust.

ACKNOWLEDGEMENTS

I would like to thank the following people for all they have done to assist me in writing Alice's story: my husband, Jim, who called "Dibs!" at the most relevant time in this process; my son, Kevin, for all his technical assistance and patience; my brother, David Matthews, for his being there for bouncing ideas off of and just being there to talk to; all my Matthews cousins, especially Dr. John Caldwell, Annie Kelly, and Beth Simon, who have shared photos, stories, and materials that have brought Alice's story to life. I would also like to thank my cousin, Carolyn Parmi, nurse extraordinaire, for always encouraging me and for sharing her experiences and her conversations with Aunt Alice; Feiga Weiss, librarian and archivist at The Zekelman Holocaust Center, Farmington Hills, Michigan for her help in gathering information and materials about Alice; and finally, my friend, Jeannie Gallimore for her love of books and assistance in proofreading this book.